Directing Game Animation

The best character animation has a strong creative intent, driving a compelling performance. With the addition of interactivity, game animation adds complexity to the craft in how best to balance art, design and technology to realize a character's performance. As a director, you are responsible for not only defining a vision for how those should balance but also being a leader, mentor and advocate for your team. But in a field of rapid iteration of ideas and techniques, that strong creative intent can be easily lost or sacrificed if not properly fostered and defined.

Directing Game Animation: Building a Vision and a Team with Intent breaks down the process of creating an intentional animation vision that can be both unique and flexible. From defining the high-level experience to breaking down tech needs, projecting a team size and empowering everyone to work together, this book will help you to fully wrap your mind around a project's animation needs.

Animation, like every part of a game, cannot succeed—let alone function—in a vacuum. This book looks to foster a discussion around the process, needs and benefits of an empowered animation team and its vision as a universal benefit for the entire industry.

This book is a guide to answering some of the most common questions people encounter when engaging with the overlap between creative and project leadership.

- **What is your role?** Learn how to establish expectations and needs specific to the project and team.

- **How do you establish a vision?** Learn how to better define and communicate creative topics such as a cohesive character performance and animation style.

- **How do you build a team?** Learn how to establish early on the team structure, skills and workflows needed to deliver on the needs of the project.

- **How do you balance creative and production needs?** Learn how to define quality, reviews and approvals in a way that empowers creativity and decision-making.

Mike Jungbluth is an animation director and game developer who has been working in games since 2006. He has worked on a variety of games, including *South of Midnight, Dragon Age: Dreadwolf, Anthem, Agents of Mayhem, Middle Earth, Shadow of Mordor* and *Call of Duty: Black Ops.* Fostering the growth of an inclusive game animation community, advocating for open sharing of industry knowledge and pushing for the importance of creative intent are his driving passions. To that end, he has created the Animation Exchange and the GDC Animation Summit, co-created the AnimState network and has spoken at GDC as well as various international conferences. His writing has been featured on GameDeveloper.com and GameIndustry.biz.

Designed cover image: Lana Bachynski

First edition published 2024
by CRC Press
2385 NW Executive Center Drive, Suite 320, Boca Raton FL 33431

and by CRC Press
4 Park Square, Milton Park, Abingdon, Oxon, OX14 4RN

CRC Press is an imprint of Taylor & Francis Group, LLC

© 2024 Mike Jungbluth

ISBN: 9781032410876 (hbk)
ISBN: 9781032410784 (pbk)
ISBN: 9781003356196 (ebk)

DOI: 10.1201/9781003356196

Typeset in Minion
by codeMantra

Access the Support Material: www.routledge.com/9781032410784

Directing Game Animation
Building a Vision and a Team with Intent

Mike Jungbluth

CRC Press
Taylor & Francis Group
Boca Raton London New York

CRC Press is an imprint of the
Taylor & Francis Group, an **informa** business

Contents

Foreword

Mike Jungbluth

Animation, as an art form, is often seen as an opportunity to bring to life anything that could be imagined. And animators are often seen as either goofy jesters or bleary-eyed artists toiling over the most minute details. But like any craft, the reality is that it is a mix of creativity, training, observation and execution that allows the impossible to be made possible. And when it is part of a commercial media creation, there is additional tension between that artistic craft and the production realities to finish and release that creation as soon as possible. It is the combination of all those factors that defines the vision, quality and consistency of the animation. And some of those areas are better understood and examined than others.

There are a great number of books,[1] schools and videos[2] that teach the craft of animation and how it can be applied to different mediums and genres. This book is not one of those that will teach you how to animate. This book is about what you should do when you are in charge of a team of people focused on animation.

Likewise, there are already books[3] that discuss being a director for animated films, which can also have applications to other mediums. But what this book is focused on is directing animation specifically for video games, which, although might seem narrowly focused, makes it all the more necessary to focus on. Because, as far as I can tell, this is the first book or resource entirely dedicated to the topic. And there is very much a need for it.

Since 2020, I have helped to run the *AnimState of the Industry Survey*,[4] which asks game animation professionals from around the world to anonymously share their thoughts and experiences in regard to the work they do. One of the largest and most consistent findings is that job satisfaction is

	Industry Struggles	Studio Struggles	
Capture	1%	3%	Capture
Compensation	17%	10%	Compensation
Creative	9%	8%	Creative
Culture	16%	6%	Culture
Hiring	9%	14%	Hiring
Knowledge Sharing	12%	12%	Knowledge Sharing
Leadership	9%	9%	Leadership
Outsource	4%	3%	Outsource
Production	15%	18%	Production
Tech	10%	18%	Tech

STUDIO AND INDUSTRY STRUGGLES

FIGURE 0.1 A chart showing the most common studio and industry struggles, derived from the responses of the 2021 AnimState of the industry survey.

most driven by trust in leadership, a clear path for career growth, proper training and a strong work/life balance. Along with that, *Production Issues* are the top concern people regularly cite as both an industry issue and a studio issue (Figure 0.1).

At the same time, the clearest path for career growth and more financial compensation is often tied to becoming a lead or director, which all makes for a perfect storm of necessity to discuss and demystify the role and responsibilities of animation direction for video games.

This book is then not only for current or aspiring animation directors but also for anyone in a leadership role that incorporates, relies upon or influences animation. Animation, like every part of a game, cannot succeed, let alone function, in a vacuum. Discussing the process, needs and benefits of an empowered animation team and vision is a universal benefit for the industry.

WHAT DOES AN ANIMATION DIRECTOR DO?

Animation in games is a complex craft that requires a balance between art, game design, narrative and tech. As a director, you are responsible for not only defining a vision for how those should all balance but also being a leader, mentor and advocate for your team. In all of that, creative intent is at the core of what drives character animation, which can easily be lost or sacrificed if not properly fostered and defined. At any time, as an animation director, you need to be able to wear and switch between any of those hats as the project, team or your creative drive demands.

WHAT WILL BE COVERED IN THIS BOOK?

I regularly think about something George Massenburg, a sound engineer and inventor, once said during an interview[5]:

> 'You have to work from your head, your heart and your guts... you have to figure out what is common to this... that balance.'

This book is how I strive to find that balance. I will break down a process on how to create an intentional animation vision that can be both unique and flexible. From defining the high-level experience to breaking down tech needs, projecting a team size and empowering a team, this book will help you to wrap your arms around a project's animation needs and give best practices on how to then clearly present and execute on that intent with all members of the development team. This follows a chronological development approach, as if you are beginning a new project from the beginning. However, it can be applied at any stage of a development cycle, as needed. And like any creative process, this is best viewed not as an exact formula, where checking each box guarantees success, but as tools in your problem-solving toolbox for when you see the need arise on your project. The more comfortable you become in your role, the more you will be able to choose and adapt each tool to the specific needs of your team and project.

WHAT DO I KNOW ABOUT ANIMATION DIRECTION?

I have been a leading figure in game animation for over ten years now. This has manifested itself by leading in-house teams, fostering communication between studios within publisher organizations and organizing the larger game animation industry through GDC, the Animation Exchange and AnimState. This has given me the unique opportunity to learn, adapt and implement some of the best practices from multiple points of view that few others have had the chance to experience.

I originally began my animation focus in 2d animation throughout college, which gave me a very traditional mindset in terms of the fundamentals of the craft. After graduation, I learned 3d animation to land my first job as a game animator. While working across multiple generations of technology, including handheld, multiple console generations, single-player narrative experiences and online multiplayer experiences,

I became increasingly focused on the overlap of game design and animation. As I moved into senior and then lead roles, my focus was on the holistic role of animation as a form of communication in the interactive space. Across eight different studios, using different technology and workflows at each, understanding the thorough lines of creative intent, production and cross-disciplinary collaboration became a universal benefit, regardless of the team, project or resources.

From recognizing the benefit of meeting so many new people and processes as I moved to different studios and realizing a lack of industry-wide knowledge sharing in terms of interactive animation, I pitched the idea of an animation-focused summit to GDC. This resulted in the Animation Bootcamp, which first debuted in 2013. Since then, the involvement and focus of animation at GDC have grown at an exponential pace, with speakers and sessions regularly ranking as some of the highest-rated talks of the event. My experience organizing and planning the GDC talks led to working directly with Twitch to create the Animation Exchange, an independent conference entirely free and online, to share the GDC experience live with everyone around the world (Figure 0.2).

FIGURE 0.2 A picture of the 2014 GDC animation Bootcamp speakers. Back row, from left to right: Mariel Cartwright, David Rosen, Jalil Sadool, Ryan Duffin and Mike Jungbluth. Front row, from left to right: Tasha Sounart, Tim Borrelli, Jay Hosfelt, Kristjan Zadziuk and Simon Unger.

All of which led to my becoming an animation director in 2018: first at BioWare, defining an animation vision for Dragon Age that would set it apart from other games and media in the fantasy genre, and then at Compulsion Games, focusing on hand-crafted, original worlds and characters that are meant to immediately stand out, delight and surprise.

It is the culmination of all these experiences that have influenced and refined the approaches I detail in this book. Thank you for taking the time and interest in learning more about directing animation for games. I am excited to share my passion and process with you!

NOTES

1. If you have found this book, then you are almost certainly aware of these other books. But they are classics of the craft for a reason. Richard Williams' *The Animator's Survival Kit: A Manual of Methods, Principles and Formulas* (2001), Frank Thomas and Ollie Johnston's *The Illusion of Life: Disney Animation* (1981) and Walt Stanchfield's *Drawn to Life: 20 Golden Years of Disney Master Classes* (2009). And specifically for the fundamentals of game animation, Jonathan Cooper has written the definitive guide *GameAnim: Video Game Animation Explained* (2021).

2. If you are looking for videos focused on the craft of game animation, there is a wealth of knowledge to be found through the Animation Exchange, youtube.com/@animationexchange, and GDC Animation Videos.

3. If you are looking for more books on directing animation, Tony Bancroft wrote *Directing for Animation: Everything You Didn't Learn in Art School* (2013) and Ron Diamond interviewed a number of animation directors for *On Animation Set* (2020).

4. This quote from George Massenburg came from Ben Folds' podcast *Lightning Bugs: Conversations with Ben Folds* (2021). The specific episode is titled *Building the Technology of Creativity* though you should do yourself a favor and watch/listen to every episode. Every episode is focused on creativity through the lens of different skills, disciplines and crafts, and it shaped many of the thoughts I convey throughout this book.

5. While this specific data came from the *2021 AnimState of the Industry Survey Results*, this is an annual survey with the results shared as part of the Animation Exchange. As I write this, the 2023 survey results were just released, and the concerns and struggles around production persist. And the data showed that the answer isn't to add more producers. In fact, that can be a factor in more struggles. Which is to say, this is something that will take all of us to address.

CHAPTER 1

The Role and Expectations

G IVING ANY FORM OF creative direction is not so far removed from giving someone directions to a location in the world. You need to have a strong sense of where you are, understand where the person asking for direction needs to go and then clearly communicate what they should do to get there. Whenever you start a new project, no matter what phase of development it is in, before you give any directions, getting your bearings should always be your top priority. And the best way to start that is by understanding the expectations of your role. The expectations of your role are what will keep you grounded and honest and are a solid place to return to any time you feel you might be lost.

The tricky bit is that the expectations and role of an animation director can vary based on the project, the team and the director themselves. So, if you are going to build a foundation here, you need to make sure the ground you are building upon is solid and defined.

You may already have a sense of the expectations based on interviewing for the job or from working with the team for years. In either case, for each project, and whenever someone new joins the team that could influence the expectations of your role, you should make a habit of keeping these up to date. I also like to keep these posted in a place where I will regularly see them. This could be a sticky note on your monitor, on the inside cover of a notebook you keep, at the top of a task board or on your daily to-do list.

DOI: 10.1201/9781003356196-1

Wherever you tend to organize your thoughts, having your expectations included will be of continued value.

There are three sets of people you want to include in your search for expectations: the project's leadership, the animation team you will be directing and yourself. All three could have different priorities, needs and desires. And a large part of your job will be to make sure you clearly understand how all of these overlap or conflict with one another, as success can begin and end with how well these align.

PROJECT LEADERSHIP EXPECTATIONS

This set of people can best be understood as those other people in leadership you directly work alongside or report to. Depending on the studio size, project size, type of project, organization structure or general power dynamics of the team, this can be a wide or narrow net to cast. But it can be the most important, because these are the peers you will be regularly communicating with when advocating for the needs of the animation team and working to understand the needs and priorities of the project itself. This is also most likely the set of people who will give you the most varied set of responses to your expectations, based on their area of expertise and past experience with the craft of animation. This is all incredibly valuable information to define early on, though, as this will give you keen insight into future conversations you will have throughout the project around quality, complexity and available support. And beyond those purely transactional reasons, this will give you an early opportunity to get to know the values, interests and personalities of the other people driving the overall project.

This can easily grow to be a long list of people, and you might not always know the best people to include. These are generally the best people or types of roles you are looking to start with.

- *Head of the Project*

- *Head of Production*

- *Head of Design*

- *Head of Narrative*

- *Head of Tech*

- *Head of Art*
- *Head of Audio*
- *Head of the Studio*

We will discuss the potential job titles and expectations of each of those shortly. But first, let's define some important questions you should be able to answer after talking to them. *What are your expectations of an animation director?* is as clear a question as you can ask for this, and it will often give you most of what you need. But here are some valuable follow-up questions that will help you better understand any specific expectations they may have.

- *What do they hope you prioritize as an animation director?*
- *What do they think has been lacking in animation on past projects?*
- *What has them excited about animation on this current project?*
- *What part of the project do they expect to require additional attention?*
- *What is a game where they believe the animation has been successful?*
- *What is a game where they believe the animation has been a detriment to the experience?*

Being able to answer each of those questions will help you to understand their priorities, where you are most likely to find some future challenges, what excites them creatively and how they value animation as part of the full experience.

With those in mind, let's talk about some of the expected expectations from the people and roles within team leadership.

Head of the Project

This role could go by a few titles, like Creative Director, Game Director or Project Director. It might also be the Executive Producer, though we will cover them in another section. Because what you are looking for here is the person who holds and drives the creative vision of the game. The person who, when all other disciplines have competing needs or desires, makes the call on what is most important to the overall experience. Depending on what craft and background they have can very much influence their expectations of the role of an animation director. Generally, the conversation points here will revolve around supporting and driving the overall player experience, tone, style and quality of the project. As this person is where the creative buck theoretically starts and stops, it is important to make sure you have a very clear set of expectations for what they expect from the animation director. Some additional questions for this person are:

- *How high of a quality bar are they expecting?*

- *Do they expect a high consistency of quality or a varied consistency of quality to support more novelty?*

- *What are their expectations for defining a new animation vision versus maintaining a more established or conventional vision?*

- *Where do they expect there to be challenges on the project in terms of animation?*

All of this will be necessary information to establish and understand when it comes to defining the high-level vision of animation for the game, what areas they are likely to ask you to prioritize or focus on and the creative support you should expect when realizing any of this.

Head of Production

This is most likely going to be the Executive Producer or Lead Producer. The person you are looking for here is the person who is driving the production process, schedule and budget. This is very important to understand, as it will inform you of the resources and timeline you have to deliver on the creative vision of the game. Some valuable questions to ask this person are:

- *What sort of team size is expected?*

- *What is the expected structure of the team?*

- *What is the expected amount of time for pre-production, production and post-production?*

- *What are the expectations around the amount of outsourcing planned?*

- *How much budget or support for training or new software can be expected?*

All of this information will help you to understand the time and resources you will have available to deliver on the creative vision being established.

Head of Design

This could be the Design Director, Game Director, Gameplay Director or some other position that says Design in the title. Ultimately, you are looking for the person who holds the vision for overall game design on the project and ultimately balances all of the design departments and features of the project. And like with the Head of the Project, what discipline of design they come from can very much influence their expectations and answers to the following questions:

- *What are the expected features of the game?*
- *What are the primary verbs in the game?*
- *What games are you expecting to compete with?*
- *Do you expect features to be more focused on breadth or depth?*
- *Who is the expected player base that the project is being designed for?*
- *How are playtests, user research and analytics expected to be used in the development process?*

The person in this role may be one of the most important persons to establish a strong relationship and foundation of trust with on the entire project. The scope of work, the iterative process, when to move from prototype to polish and how much animation will be seen as a partner or service provider very much depend on supporting and managing the expectations established here. There will be a lot of back and forth here as the game moves through the stages of production, so it is important to always check on this person's expectations and if you are living up to them, as they can very much evolve over time.

Head of Narrative

The role you are looking for here is likely Narrative Director, Lead Writer or Lead Narrative Designer. This is the person who is driving the narrative vision of the game and will certainly give a lot of clarity around the expectations of the characters and the world you will be helping to breathe life into. Some questions that will very quickly come up here are:

- *What is the expected tone of the game?*

- *What narrative systems are expected? (cutscenes, scripted moments, banter, etc.)*

- *What are the expectations around verbal and non-verbal communication needs?*

- *What are the expected narrative priorities?*

- *What languages are expected to be supported for localization?*

Along with design, narrative plays a major role in defining the scope, and work animation will need to help realize the project. The characters and worlds often start from the minds of the narrative team, and it is incredibly important that animation be in constant and regular communication with the narrative team. The expectations and involvement of the animation director in the narrative process can vary depending on other roles on the team, such as Cinematic Director, Performance Director and Realization Director. But at the very least, having a strong understanding of the narrative and tone of the game is required to maintain consistency in character performances and tone across all aspects of the game.

Head of Art

This is likely to be the Art Director, who is generally the other person in project leadership that most people will connect to the craft of animation. This is natural, as art shares a long history with the craft of animation in games. Until more recent console generations, animation was often a part of the art department, with generalists responsible for animation on top of other crafts. And within smaller teams, this can still be the case. But it is important to not take this connection for granted and assume the expectations of the Head of Art match your own, as they will likely be coming from different expertise in terms of character and environment, 2d or 3d. All of which can vary in their specific interests, focus and biases. Some additional questions that can be valuable to understand in terms of art are:

- *What is the expected art style of the project?*

- *What are the games that art is setting as competitive benchmarks?*

- *What part of the art direction do they expect people to most recognize?*

- *What are your expectations and vision for vfx?*

Due to the history of art and animation being so connected, the biggest expectations you are looking for are the style and quality bar being set by the other visual crafts, so that you know what animation needs to match. It doesn't matter how great a model looks or how well an environment is staged and lit if its movement, style and tone don't match.

Head of Tech

This could be the Technical Director, Engineering Director, Lead Programmer or some other role that is focused on driving the technical needs and process of the project. When it comes to the engine being used, workflows, debugging tools and programming support, this is the person who is focused on making sure the project is technically viable. Often times, this person will have a good high-level vision of the areas with the most technical risk and what the project priorities will be in terms of optimizing existing technology and workflows versus supporting new features and workflows. Some tech-specific questions to be able to answer are:

- *How regularly do we expect to integrate engine updates?*

- *Which areas of the animation pipeline do you expect to need the most support?*

- *How much of the runtime budget do you expect to be available to animation?*

- *Is there a runtime budget allotted for CPU and GPU?*

- *What is the tech debt you expect to most impact animation?*

Technical decisions made at the beginning of the project, such as the choice of the engine, online architecture and programming priorities, can have the most long-term impact on your team, and any subsequent changes to these decisions may require a non-trivial amount of time to change. Understanding the focus and reality of the programming department will let you know where you can expect technology to answer future challenges. And where can you expect changes in workflows that might most impact your team? Because of the specific importance required to understand all of this, we will discuss how to define your unique tech needs in Chapter 4.

Head of Audio

Here you are most likely looking for the Audio Director, Audio Lead or Lead Sound Designer. In most cases, animation is downstream of other disciplines, but audio is one of the disciplines that is downstream from animation. And because of that, it is important to understand the needs and priorities of the audio team, so that you can support them. Some good questions to keep in mind when establishing expectations with audio are:

- *What areas of the audio pipeline do you expect to need the most lead time to define?*

- *What features of the project do you expect to need a lot of focus from audio?*

- *What areas of the animation workflow do you expect to cause the most challenges for audio?*

- *What expectations do you have in terms of the review and approval process?*

With audio being toward the end of the production pipeline, anything animation can do to help inform and include audio is going to be incredibly valuable to them. Thinking about them early and often will make sure you keep them in mind anytime there are proposed changes to timing or actions later in the project. Changes to animation can and will very much impact audio.

Head of Studio

This could be the studio General Manager, the CEO, or some other business or organization-focused role. Your need or ability to go in depth on role expectations here can vary depending on the size of the studio and how involved this person is with the development of the projects. This will also very much influence the expectations they will have of an animation director. Regardless of these elements, having a relationship or visibility on any level with this person can help in terms of any high-impact needs you may have. Understanding the value of animation to this person is incredibly valuable when looking at the big picture and future of the studio. Some questions to help get to that are:

- *How do they expect animation to help drive the brand of the project and studio?*

- *How do they expect animation to help drive the future of the studio?*

- *Where have they seen animation add value to a project or studio that they didn't expect?*

- *How much do they expect to be able to invest in animation on this project and the future?*

- *What do they expect a successful animation team to look like?*

As most animation directors come from an arts background, questions around business values might not come naturally to you. This makes it all the more important to build a strong relationship with people that it does naturally come to so that you can learn to trust one another on how to reach shared goals. As the Head of the Studio, this person is focused on the future of the team and projects. The more they understand and recognize what animation can bring to the table, the more they can work that into their plans and pitches.

While this is already a healthy number of people to establish expectations with, there is a good chance there are even more people you will want to talk to. As you talk to these people, you will likely find other leaders at the studio you need to establish expectations with. VFX leadership will likely be high on that list for many of the same reasons as audio. Depending on the core features and experiences intended for the game, UI and UX might be key partners you need to establish expectations with. And the larger the team or the more complex the game, there are likely additional Directors and Leads reporting to the Heads of Departments, so you will want to understand what they expect from animation. This may seem like a lot of different opinions and priorities to balance. But these will be necessary to Understanding Project Needs in Chapter 2, which can then help you prioritize all of these expectations along with the expectations of this next group.

ANIMATION TEAM EXPECTATIONS

The expectations here are more likely to match your own, so there are likely fewer surprises to find here. That said, it is still important to talk to each member of the team you will be directing. And for this, the wider the definition of what the team includes, the better. Not only animators should be part of this but also technical animators, animation programmers, animation system designers, cinematic designers and anyone else who directly contributes to or creates animation and animated sequences in the game. These are the people you support and advocate for, so it is imperative that you know with clarity what they expect and need from you. No matter the title, seniority or experience, spend the time to talk to each person to define the expectations they have of you. Depending on the person, simply asking *What are your expectations of an animation director?* can elicit a lot of thoughts. Or, it may result in silence, as they may not have explicitly thought about it before. In both cases, having a few more specific questions can help:

- *What is something you valued in previous animation directors or leads you worked with?*
- *What is something that frustrated you about previous animation directors or leads you worked with?*
- *What most excites you about the current project?*
- *What most frustrates you about current processes?*
- *What does a successful animation team look like to you?*
- *What does a successful project look like to you?*
- *What does a successful career look like to you?*

Some of these questions go beyond establishing their expectations of you and overlap with areas you will want to focus on with them in terms of mentorship and empowerment, which we will discuss in Chapter 12. But even in those cases, knowing what they are looking for in the work they will do on the project and how they want to grow their career will very much play into their expectations of you. Because helping them find success in those areas is very much an expectation of the Animation Director role.

Like Project Leadership expectations, it is important to establish these with anyone new to your team. This will be half exploratory to make sure you understand their expectations of you, but also for you to lay out the established expectations of the animation director role. This is something that can be done during the interview or onboarding process. Likely, the more senior the new team member, the more specific interest they will have in understanding and establishing all of this, which could have come up during the interview. Otherwise, it is fine to convey this as part of the onboarding experience, so that they know what your priorities and focus are likely to be.

YOUR EXPECTATIONS

After you have talked to everyone necessary to understand the expectations they are placing on you as Animation Director, it is important for you to be honest about your own expectations of the role. A large part of a leadership role is always focused on supporting the team, but there is certainly a core part that requires you to have your own vision and convictions on what is needed from your role. You are likely in this role because you have a keen understanding of the value and opportunity afforded by empowering a stronger animation team and vision. On top of that, you also probably have specific expertise within animation, be it gameplay, cinematics or tech. So then, the trick here is to understand your personal expectations and how to balance those with the expectations from the team, project and studio.

From all of this, you should get a sense of priorities based on how often the same point is brought up. If you have questions about priorities, it is good to follow up with the Head of the Project or Discipline Expert best suited to understand the specific needs and goals of the expectations.

Something I have found to be incredibly useful in finding a way to balance all of this is by using this chart of Interaction Design, as described by Bill Verplank.[1] His approach is to think of the person experiencing the creation at the center of the creation, and then each of the disciplines or groups involved in the creation is based on how they relate to the person at the center. This starts with the input and display device the person is using to engage with the experience, which then defines the groups or disciplines involved in the process of communicating information to and from the person at the center of the experience (Figure 1.1).

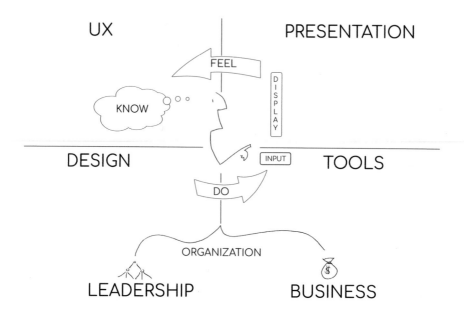

FIGURE 1.1   A diagram depicting the multi-discipline flow of interactive design. Originally designed by Bill Verplank though I have slightly modified it with labels to specify which areas of game development it is speaking to.

For our purposes, start by placing each of the expectation points you have from others within the different sections of this chart. Then, add or highlight any points that match your own personal expectations. With this, you can visually understand the high-level expectations of your role and what that will mean for you. This is incredibly valuable to know when it comes to seeing how your expectations match those of the rest of the team's and what portion of the experience you will be most involved in.

I personally gravitate towards the Design, Presentation and Leadership sections of this chart, so having expectations from the team and project that align with that will make for a natural fit. If I were on a team or project that expected the Animation Director role to be more focused on the Tech, UX or Business side of things, I would be less naturally suited to meet the expectations. In which case, a top priority for me would be finding people I can rely upon and trust in the Tech, UX and Business sections to educate and cover my blind spots. This will very much influence your team structure, which will be covered in Chapter 5.

It may also be that once you see the expectations of the team and compare them with your own, this isn't actually the opportunity or fit you are looking for. It can be hard to turn down an opportunity to direct a team, but it is important to know that taking on a role like this would be a disservice to yourself and the team. Being able to identify that early shows a level of responsibility and awareness that will suit you well for future opportunities.

With all of this now in hand, you should have a starting point for where you need to focus most in your role. If any of the above chapter callouts feel like an immediate priority to your needs, then jumping to those sections is a good next step. Otherwise, the next step on the director's path is understanding the specific needs of the project.

NOTE

1 While this specific graph comes from Bill Verplank's *Interaction Design Sketchbook* (2009), his entire website has wonderfully explained and illustrated philosophies around interactive design and cross-disciplinary collaboration. https://www.billverplank.com/IxDSketchBook.pdf

CHAPTER 2

Understanding the Project Vision

A NIMATION IS AN ART of communicating intent. The intent of a character. The world. The artist. And for games, that means before you can establish a strong animation vision, you need to understand the intent of every part of the project. It is the narrative, design, art, audio and animation that all come together to define and communicate the intent of the characters, the world, the development team and the player. Any animation direction that is established that isn't aligned to the core intent of those key areas will quickly find itself out of step with the rest of the project, no matter how visually compelling or unique it may be. Your animation vision needs to be resilient enough to absorb the tweaks and adjustments that happen through development. The more aligned the animation vision is with the core vision of these upstream disciplines, short of their core vision changing, the animation direction can remain flexible to iteration while remaining consistent overall.

Noticeably absent from the above visions is Tech. Which is very critical to defining any animation vision. Critical enough that it will be the focus of Chapter 4. But understanding the creative vision of Design, Narrative and Art will very much influence the needs, priorities and support available from the project's tech team.

Let us look over the sort of vision documents and concepts you are likely to find in each of the other disciplines and the sort of information

DOI: 10.1201/9781003356196-2

you will want to highlight as reference points for crafting the animation vision. After the Creative Vision, there is no specific or best order to follow in terms of the other disciplines. And most likely, you will find yourself moving back and forth as each discipline continues to define and explore its own visions. It is best here to be a sponge for any and all information and inspiration you are going to uncover. Take lots of notes and highlight areas of interest or repeating themes you see across the disciplines that you will be able to refer to when defining the animation style and tone, discussed in Chapters 6 and 7.

UNDERSTANDING THE CREATIVE VISION

This is the high-level vision that is intended to bind together all of the different disciplines. Depending on the background of the Head of the Project, what you find as the driving vision here could be anything from a single-sentence vision statement to a series of concept pieces or in-depth presentations. Immersing yourself in all of those is key to creatively aligning yourself with the heart of the project. But there are a couple of very specific things you want to be clear on before approaching the other discipline visions to find your own creative line.

Genre

What is the genre of the game you are making? Action? Adventure? Simulation? Puzzle? A hybrid of a few? Knowing very clearly the intended genre is the first step towards understanding the intended audience you are focusing your experience on. And there is always a core, intended audience. Even if you are going for as broad an appeal as possible, if you try to make something for everyone, you have made nothing for anyone. The best creations are ones that feel personally crafted to connect the people making them to the people engaging with them. This starts by being honest about the genre and audience of the game so that you can speak authentically to them with your full heart.

Tone

The tone of the game is as important as the genre. Is it serious? Is it ridiculous? Is it self-aware? Is it allegorical? Does it have a mix or range of tones? Like the genre, this will help dictate the audience you are going to focus on. But it will also help you understand how much of your own personal tastes align with the creative vision of the game. Depending on your interests, some tones may be a more natural fit for your specific sensibilities than others. It is important to be very conscious of this so that you can keep your own tonal bias in check. Or allow it to run carefree without abandon.

Platforms

How will people engage with your project? On a large screen? On a small screen? VR? A controller? Mouse and keyboard? Touch screen? Body motion? The impact of this decision will have significant technical implications, which we will discuss in Chapter 4, but it will also give you an understanding of the scale and standards that are likely to be expected by both the team and the audience.

Player Fantasy

A good lens to view the creative vision of the game and stay in the proper headspace of the intended audience is by understanding the intended player fantasy. This is where the genre and tone should align with and be reflected by the various discipline visions. Is the fantasy one of redemption? Romance? Power? Building? Failure? Should the player feel smart? Are they an agent of chaos? This is not only their stated and intended objectives but also how they are meant to feel while engaging with the experience. Should they feel like an adored hero on a quest to save their way of life? Are they being pushed against the odds to combat invading forces? Are they working to balance a community alongside the ever-depleting resources of the land? Maybe they are desperately trying to convince an uncaring god over a cup of coffee?

Having a clear understanding of the player's fantasy will be a valuable lens not just for engaging with each discipline's vision but also incredibly valuable to use as you get into Technical Needs (Chapter 4), Performance (Chapter 6), Style (Chapter 7), Scope (Chapter 10) and Feedback (Chapter 11). All of this makes it incredibly important to make sure the entire Project Leadership is aligned with what that player fantasy is.

With this understanding of the genre, tone, platforms and player fantasy, you are now better aligned to engage with each specific discipline's vision. Having these always in mind will help you keep track of a consistent through line as you dive into an ocean of creative opportunities, ideas and interests.

UNDERSTANDING THE DESIGN VISION

While the role and expectations of design can vary from studio and project, what is consistent is that they define the functional intent of the experience. Art, Animation and Narrative then give that function its form. Depending on the project and team, there is potential for a lot of different design vision documents, presentations and prototypes you will likely need to dig through. After discussing the expectations of your role with the Head of Design on your project, you will most likely have a good idea of the priorities and areas they will be most focused on. Often times, that will be the core of the project itself, but it can just as well be the area with the greatest number of unknowns that could see the most iteration and changes. Understanding the solid core and foundation of the design versus novelty or risky innovation will be important to what you want to use as the basis of the animation vision.

Design Docs

Design documents come in many forms. They can be dense design bibles that try to list out every feature in detail. They could be one-sheet briefs that contain a problem statement and testing requirements to validate success. They could be vision boards or presentation videos. They could be sheets filled with metrics and graphs. They could be a few random thoughts or notes jotted down on a shared page. You are likely to find any mix of these, as different designers and areas of design will naturally lean toward one method over another. Ideally, the Head of Design is curating all of these documents and checking them against the high-level design vision. But often, these are being created faster than anyone can keep track of or organize them, so they are best viewed as thoughts representing a moment in time. And when viewed holistically, you can get a sense of the consistent theme and intent of each part of the design. What follows in this section are the key elements you are looking for to see and understand the big picture of the design's intent.

Core Features

These features are the foundation upon which the experience is built. Some projects may only have one core feature. Some may have many. But what defines these is that if the feature were to be removed from the game, it would change the type of game you are making. Examples of this would be multi-player or single player. Open world or linear levels. Turn-based or real-time combat. Defined characters or customizable characters. Linear narratives or branching narratives. Methods of traversal. These define the systems and verbs that design will be using to construct the experience of the game. And these are what the team will likely spend the majority of their effort on. As you go through documents and have conversations with people on the team, take note of the features people talk about the most and plan to rely on the most. These are the elements of the project you do not want to lose sight of, because if they change at all, there is bound to be ripples in any vision and work the team will be focused on. And these are the features you will most need to verify against tech needs and quality standards when it comes time to prototype and fully realize.

It is also important to understand who is the point of contact or vision holder for each of these features. Much like talking to different team members to understand their expectations of your role, you will want to understand the expectations of the person driving that feature. How they interpret the needs of the feature and the way it fits in with the rest of the experience will be crucial when further breaking down how best to support it. And also, like role expectations, if someone new takes over as the person in charge of a feature, you will want to verify that previously established expectations are still valid.

Once you have confirmed the core feature list with the Head of Design and Head of the Project, keep that list nearby. You will be returning to it so that you can directly reference it in terms of breaking down tech needs and the core animation vision.

Secondary Features

These are features that are meant to add some novelty or breadth to the experience, but they do not require the same depth as a core feature. These are likely not central to the core needs of the game, and if feature cuts need to be made, these are the most likely candidates. It isn't always clear which features may be primary or secondary, so let's look at an example.

Traversal can be either a primary or secondary feature, depending on the project or genre. If platforming or exploration are primary features, then traversal actions like sprinting, jumping and mantling are most likely considered a big part of that primary feature. A large part of the second-to-second gameplay likely revolves around using those as core actions. But if combat or rpg systems are the primary features of your project, then traversal is likely a secondary feature. It exists as either an additional combo action for combat or as a novelty action to give minor agency to players running from objective to objective.

Ideally, if something is a secondary feature, that would also mean it is not complex to support and realize. But depth and complexity are not always the same thing. This means, much like with core features, you will want to work with the person driving this feature to understand the specific needs required. That way, when you work to define the vision and tech requirements needed to support it, you aren't putting in the effort to build a spaceship when what you need is a skateboard.

Player Fantasy Features

What you are looking for here is an understanding of which design features specifically speak to the core of the player's fantasy. Generally, the Core Features are the ones that most reflect the player's fantasy, but it is important to understand which Secondary Features also reflect it. Those will be powerful opportunities to lean into the Tone, as well as strong candidates to prioritize higher than others when it comes to future support. Something that may feel like a novelty to the experience may actually be something that can very much strengthen and convey the player's fantasy in an important way. Understanding that specific need and value will help you devise presentation solutions that can deliver on the need in the best way possible. Sometimes that could be more depth to the feature, or sometimes it could be removing the complexity of the system and leaning toward a bolder visual presentation.

These have a chance of being opportunities to further strengthen design and animation relationships, as well as become lightning rods of conflicting prioritizations. These can often blur the line between wants and needs, as the value can be subjective to the person or discipline. Recognizing these features early is incredibly important so that these conversations can establish as clear expectations as possible from everyone involved. This will allow you to know how much you should expect to invest in or lean upon these features, through the lens of the player's fantasy, when it comes to communicating and executing on the animation vision.

Comparative Experiences

Each discipline often references other creations as a conversational shorthand when discussing their own creations. And for designers, this is often other games. It is incredibly common to have specific features, characters, levels or moments from other games used as design references in conversations. Which means you need to either play, watch or read up on other games that exist within the same genre or space as the one you are making. This is important for a couple of reasons.

The first reason is to, of course, understand what the design is referencing at the moment. This allows the conversation to stay in the moment without regularly stopping the person from explaining something there is expected to be a shared understanding of. There will still be times when someone references something especially niche or unique to their own experience that will require additional explanation. But in terms of the major titles or creations residing in a similar space as your own, having a foundational knowledge of the other games is a base-level expectation for your role.

The second reason is so that you are able to separate the functional reference point being brought up from the visual form it takes within the game. And you can then follow up immediately as to the design intent. This is valuable on a macro and micro level. Let's use the genre of an action rpg to provide examples of each.

A macro example would be when different melee combat systems are being discussed and both *God of War* and *Shadow of Mordor* are brought up. With knowledge of both, you can immediately understand the key differences implied and what that would mean in terms of design intent and animation support. *God of War* uses a melee system based on branching player combos, with different enemy reactions based on the success of completing those combos. This makes it similar to having a variety of different melodies available to play, and the player is choosing which they think is best for that moment. *Shadow of Mordor* uses a more free-form approach, where instead of performing specific combos, you are continuously linking a suite of contextual attacks to maintain an endless flow state. This would be less about playing specifically defined melodies and more of a jam session. Knowing the differences between these two combat systems will immediately give you some indication of how mobile the player is meant to be, high-level enemy behaviors that may be required, the importance of secondary abilities to the player, the number of enemies in an encounter and more. Those are the areas you want to be able to dig into deeper in a design discussion, as opposed to focusing on how the characters, attacks or weapons may look.

As a more micro example, if someone were to say, 'like Link's jump down thrust attack' you can immediately picture in your head the functional purpose of the action being referenced, separate from the action

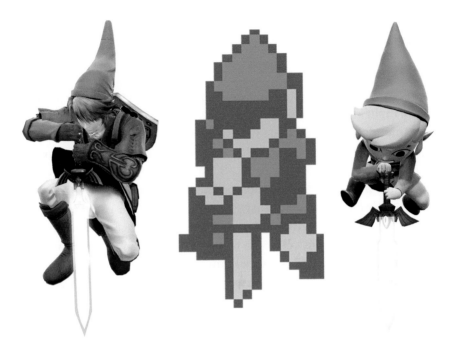

FIGURE 2.1 A picture depicting Legend of Zelda's Link performing his jump-down thrust attack with a sword, across various depictions of the character. Copyright Nintendo.

of the animation itself. In this case, they are likely looking for a downward drop attack that has the character quickly plummet to the ground to attack a single target below them. Or, to be put even more succinctly, 'a single target strike on an enemy below' (Figure 2.1).

Being able to immediately grasp that in the moment is key because it allows you to understand the functional design need being discussed and break it down in a way that is separate from the form of the action. Because the form of the action how it looks could be conveyed in a number of different ways that could be much better suited to the character you are all developing.

In Chapter 10, we will discuss in more detail how to further clarify function from form in a way that balances creative vision and production needs. A fair number of design and animation communication issues can happen when the function and form are not clearly defined between the two groups. So spending the time to develop a deep understanding of other games is crucial to having substantive discussions between design and animation.

Game Feel

This speaks to how the game responds to the player. This is the combination of input and feedback driving the feel of the interactive experience. Is the game a fast-paced shooter? Is it a methodical simulation of an activity or sport? How a game feels to play is at the center of where design and animation overlap.

Luckily, there is an entire book on the topic, *Game Feel: A Designer's Guide to Virtual Sensation*,[1] that everyone involved in game animation should read and regularly reference. It breaks down common points of contention, like responsiveness, in wonderfully clear and concrete ways. It gives you a vocabulary to engage with metrics and metaphor in a way that will be incredibly valuable as you work to balance the look and feel of the player experience.

Being able to understand and speak confidently about the feel of the game will allow you to understand how and when animations can and should be interrupted or uninterrupted. When something is best suited to be animation-driven or physics-driven. Having a clear understanding of the game feel will be a core component that defines the needs of your animation system, which we will discuss in Chapter 4.

Game Camera

One of the 12 principles of animation is, of course, staging. Which makes the game camera an immediately important aspect of the experience to understand and help clarify. Is the game played in 3rd person or 1st person? If 3rd person, is it from behind, on the side, above, or in front of the player character? Where in the frame is the player character? How large or small is the player character in the frame? What is the field of view of the camera? Does the character's facing direction always match the camera's facing direction? How much of that is variable? Is that variable in real time or through a menu? How does the game camera transition from menus and cinematics?

All of these answers will have important and long-lasting impacts on the animation vision and scope of the project. Yet, based on the type of game and size of the team, how much attention or support the camera receives can vary. So it is important to work with design to clarify the people and constraints involved in making decisions in regards to the game camera. Even changes to the above questions that may seem minor can have significant ripples in both scope and presentation.

Taking the time to discuss camera logic, processes, workflows, reviews and approvals is something all disciplines will benefit from. The focus in Chapter 10 on Production Processes and Chapter 11 on Feedback, Reviews and Approvals will be especially applicable when it comes to collaborating on the game camera.

World Construction

In terms of the design vision, I am using world construction to include level design, mission design and even narrative design. All of which can have variable and overlapping responsibilities depending on the team and project. But ultimately, what you are looking for here is an understanding of how the world is being built and how the characters are intended to live within it. Because it is ultimately the world building that gives context to how the features are used within the realized player experience.

The size and scale of the levels will impact the size and scale of the characters. And how the characters will need to move to navigate through the space, both for gameplay and cinematics. You may need different versions of models based on gameplay and cinematic needs. The density of objects and characters will also influence character navigation and expectations around how reactive characters should be. The objectives of levels and missions can inform the different actions and verbs that need to be available to characters. There can also be a number of objects or props in the world, like doors, levers, tentacles or alien devices, that could need animation support. Generally, this is an area that animation hasn't traditionally been as involved with in game development, but it is becoming more common and necessary for games at larger scales and budgets.

This is also where you will get a sense of how much of the narrative intent is meant to happen outside of cinematics. Will there be scripted events, also known as in game cutscenes? Will there be staged scenes requiring unique character behaviors? Are they intended to be system-driven or handcrafted? Often times, all of these will require some significant tech support to create pipelines and workflows to do this at any sort of scale. Knowing that these are part of the experience is important, as it will certainly be something you want to include them in your technical breakdown as part of Chapter 4.

The Player Experience

Once you have a clear understanding of all the intended design ingredients, this is where you can take a step back and look at the fully intended player experience. Both from the beginning of the game and also during a general play session. Let's first look at the beginning of the game.

How does the game start? How long is the player in menus or cinematics before having control of a character? What is the intensity of the starting experience? What does the onboarding experience look like, in terms of tutorials and available features? Which characters or part of the world does the experience start with? All of this will help you to understand future priorities for scoping in Chapter 10, but also how much iteration is likely to happen, as discussed in Chapter 11.

Once the experience transitions from the start of the game, it is important to understand the general game loops, as that will be where players spend the majority of their time. And for that, it can be valuable to break this down into second-to-second, minute-to-minute and hour-to-hour loops. Those amounts of time are generally used by design to quantify what the player experience is intended to be at any moment, so it is a valuable framework to understand as the animation director.

Second-to-second loops are generally focused on a single feature. These are the specific actions and verbs used in combat, traversal, object interactions, mini games, etc. Game feel drives the second-to-second loops. Animators can often get caught up in this loop, as that is where it is easiest and clearest to see the individual elements being created and how they work alongside one another. This is certainly still important to you as a director, but you will want to make sure you are able to easily zoom in and out from this level to the larger loops of time.

Minute-to-minute loops are all about the transitions between features. What is the experience of specifically moving from game play sections of the experience to cinematics? How do characters in the world engage with the player when previously engaged in ambient behavior? What happens when the player spawns or respawns in the world? What all of this generally means for animation is the need to understand the connective tissue between the features and how that is intended to be presented or realized.

These can have significant implications for technical needs in Chapter 4 and scope impact in Chapter 10, as not all features are created to integrate well with one another. So having a clear understanding of what features need to fit with one another will be key to understanding the reality of supporting minute-to-minute loops.

Hour-to-hour loops are generally the place someone coming from animation has spent the least amount of time before moving into a director role. And depending on the type of experience being created, how involved the animation director needs to be can vary. The questions that happen in this loop can feel rather disconnected from the animation. What is the total balance of how long players spend in each feature? How are player objectives established and resolved? Is the mission structure defined by levels that return to a central hub or an entirely open world? The answers to all of this can start to significantly vary depending on the type of player and features available. Some players may choose to engage with one feature more than another. Some may enjoy playing at a slower pace to soak up every aspect of the experience. Others may enjoy trying to move through the world and experience it as quickly as possible as a test of their skill and mastery of the features. This is where taking the time to understand the audience becomes especially valuable. Understanding who your core audience is will help inform the conversation and direction given at this level.

If you are looking for a more actionable approach to understanding hour-to-hour loops in terms of animation support, then there is a solid go-to question you can always ask.

'How Much of This Is Intended to Happen in Menus or in the Game World?'

This can help you understand all of the features and elements of the loop. At which point you can then use the lens of audience expectations to help guide the intended direction and suggest the different ways animation can help support the overall experience.

There are also day-to-day, month-to-month and year-to-year loops, which are a big part of live service games. But those are generally more flexible and nebulous until the core experience is closer to being completed. And while those are important to keep in mind, especially when it comes to alpha, beta and launch, trying to take those into account in a core vision beyond needing to know they will exist is putting the cart well ahead of the horse. Think of those more as knowing you will have future extensions you will want to make to your vision. Making sure you have room to grow and evolve is the key when it comes to these longer loops.

UNDERSTANDING THE NARRATIVE VISION

Narrative within an interactive experience takes form in two distinct ways. The narrative the development team crafts and the narrative the players experience and influence. Animation needs to understand both sides of that conversation as one of the primary tools used to convey the visual language and performance needed to communicate a clear story. This makes narrative and design two sides of the same coin. And in terms of animation, every effort should be made to have one inform the other for a consistent performance and realization. Animation can be a glue that helps bind the design and the narrative across multiple gameplay features and narrative systems.

It is also worth your time to read some books focused on writing for games and narrative design.[2] Writing is a skill that many people think they are naturally able to understand, which can make people undervalue the real effort and skill that goes into it.

Narrative Theme

What you are looking for here is whether there is some overarching message that the narrative is conveying. For a lot of games, that may look like something straightforward, like Good vs Evil. But that is often only surface level, and if you talk to the writers, there is almost certainly more going on with the theme. Is it an allegory for free will vs fate? Overcoming oppression? Power and corruption?

It is important to understand and differentiate the theme from the tone. You can have a serious or powerful theme but a humorous or even silly tone. People don't need or even especially appreciate when a theme or message is obvious. Knowing how you can mix, match and leverage the theme from the tone will allow you to control how subtle or obvious the message is at any given moment. There are few things as powerful as subverting expectations, but in order to do so successfully, you need to understand the expectations.

Narrative Devices

There are a number of ways the narrative can be realized in the game. Everything from cutscenes to progression systems can be used to convey a narrative. What is meant here by narrative devices are the explicit narrative systems and tools being used to convey the developer-driven narrative. These are things like cutscenes, in-game scripted moments, conversation systems, ambient life, banter and player interactions. While these are generally well understood by the team at large, the specifics can be deceivingly complex or unclear the larger the team gets. Generally, the realization of these requires the cross-collaboration of writers, designers and artists that can be split across teams focused on specific areas of the game like missions, gameplay, levels and narrative. So beyond identifying the specific devices people across those teams are expecting to be used, you want to clear up a couple of things as quickly as possible.

First, you want to establish specific definitions of what any device or term specifically entails. The perception of these terms can vary by person, project or studio, so expect to spend some time investigating what is meant when discussing any of them. It can be helpful to use complexity and constraints when defining what is expected of each of these devices. Some good questions to ask when looking into these are:

- *Is the camera animated or player-controlled for these?*
- *Can this be interrupted and how?*
- *How should this react if interrupted?*
- *At what distance will these be seen?*
- *How will these be triggered in the game?*

All of these will help you understand the intent behind how they will be used and provide clarity when looking into breaking down the technical needs in Chapter 4.

After you have a clearer understanding of what devices are needed and what they entail, you will next want to have a clearer understanding of what team is expected to develop and deliver on these systems. These can often be connective tissues between features and teams, which means support for these can often fall through the cracks. Which will then likely result in these becoming new requests later in development, at which point animation support will need to be diverted from cinematics or gameplay. In order to address this, if you find you have a significant need for a variety of narrative devices, it can be worthwhile to create a dedicated part of the animation team to support all of this, which will be discussed in Chapter 5.

Cinematic Style

This is an extension of the narrative devices, but specifically focused on the elements of cinematography and editing. Like any discipline, you can devote your entire career to these skills, the specifics of which can be found in a number of fantastic books.[3] What you are specifically looking for here is how the cinematic style connects to the design vision in terms of realization. Some questions here would be:

- *Is the camera language in cinematics consistent with gameplay?*

- *Is the pacing of cinematic action consistent with gameplay action?*

- *Are the intended character actions and performances consistent with gameplay?*

- *What are the intended methods of transition between cinematics and gameplay?*

Understanding how characters and cameras will behave in relation to cinematics and gameplay will help when it comes to Defining Team Structure in Chapter 5, Defining Performance and Style in Chapters 6 and 7 and Defining Production Processes in Chapters 9 and 10.

Character Profiles

Character development can take on many different forms, and you are likely to run into all sorts of narrative documents containing multi-page back stories, personality-defining quotes, lists of traits or comparisons to other established characters. This can result in either an overload of information or inconsistent information from character to character. While there is a lot of value in diving deep into characters, well beyond what is actually seen or portrayed in the game, you want to make sure there is consistency of core information as it pertains to the realization of the character in terms of animation.

A lot of the information is likely coming from the viewpoint of a writer, and what is needed in animation is more like the viewpoint of an actor. While animators and actors have different sets of skills,[4] as an animation director, you may be the first person to engage with these characters from something resembling an actor's mindset. Here are some questions to help you understand the core aspects of characters' performance in the game.

- *What is their main objective throughout the course of the experience?*

- *How do they respond to obstacles?*

- *What is their relationship with other key characters?*

- *Do they have a narrative arc or change during the experience?*

- *What personality traits would you use to describe them?*

- *How do they fit into the theme of the narrative?*

- *How do they fit into the tone of the experience?*

The answers to these questions will be valuable when you start to explore and define the character's performance in Chapter 6.

UNDERSTANDING THE ART VISION

Art and animation are at their core visual creations meant to communicate intent. This means the art vision, and the intent behind it, is likely to be informed by many of the same investigations into the design and narrative vision. But what is likely to vary is how that is interpreted by the Head of Art. What you will then want to be focused on in terms of the art vision is that specific interpretation of the experience and how it is going to be realized by the other visual art crafts.

Visual Inspiration

Artists can pull inspiration from a number of sources. Nature. Culture. Fashion. Film. Music. Theater. History. The list is endless and can be combined in any number of ways. Looking through concept art and reference boards should give you an initial idea of the main areas of inspiration. But don't stop there. Talk with the Head of Art and the Head of the Project of what creatively inspires them. It could be specific artists, films, geographic locations, cultures and belief systems, genres of music or past eras. All of those are valuable areas of inspiration that are likely to come out in both obvious and subtle ways, throughout the course of realizing the visuals of the project. Some of these may be familiar to you already, so you have a shared creative touchpoint to work from. Some of these may be new to you, which gives you a number of creative areas to research and immerse yourself in. The more you can understand what is creatively driving and inspiring the art vision, the more you can build upon or incorporate it into the animation vision, as described in Chapters 6 and 7.

With the inspiration behind the art vision understood, you can now engage with the realization of that vision in the specific visual styles being used in the project.

Character Art Style

The art style and fidelity of characters can be one of the most immediate influences on how an audience may perceive the tone of the project. Once that immediate impression happens, how those characters move will either continue or subvert that initial impression. Which means the style of the character art will most likely have one of the most clear impacts on the animation of the project. How stylized or realistic the character art is directly influences how exaggerated the physicality and expressiveness of the characters may be. Or if there could be a need for character deformation that allows for motion smears or scale. The degree to which cloth, hair and other secondary elements are incorporated into the designs will drive some technical needs to be discussed in Chapter 4. The level of detail will impact the technical art and rigging needs required to realize that detail when moving. And depending on the narrative needs of the game, how the style relates to faces will play a major factor in how successful the facial animation will be.

The higher the quality of the character art, the higher the expectations are for the motion of the characters to match that. Seeing and establishing examples that represent the intended execution of the character art style will help as you focus on technical needs in Chapter 4, team structure in Chapter 5 and the overall animation style in Chapter 7.

VFX Style

VFX, like animation, sits in between a number of crafts and collaborators. They are influenced by the color and shape language of the art style. They are responsible for communicating design and feedback in ways no other visual discipline can. And they are one of the disciplines throughout the course of development that are downstream of animation. So it is important to talk with the Head of VFX to understand the specific style, vision and expected needs of the project. Are they planning the vfx to be more realistic or stylized? What are some examples of a similar vfx style they are aiming for? These will be important to have some understanding of when it comes to defining tech needs and team structure in the coming chapters.

Environment Art Style

While the major focus of animation departments is often on characters, it is becoming more and more important that the world also move and respond to convey the intent of the developers and players. Often, it is a mix of environment artists, tech artists, physic engineers, rendering engineers, lighting artists and level designers that have been responsible for that movement in games, as the complexity of that movement has been limited. But as art visions and intent grow, the need for animation to have visibility in that work becomes important. And while inanimate objects moving are generally less complex than characters, the workflows and pipelines for how that can happen are not generally the same between the two.

It is also important to understand how the art style of the world influences character movement and interactions. Objects that may look appropriate for a game camera may not work well for cinematics. Any part of the world that expects to have characters regularly interacting with the art, such as chairs, cups, levers and doors, is worth chatting about early in terms of gameplay and narrative needs.

All of this is required to understand the art style of the environment, the expectations for how it will move and how the characters and objects will respond to one another. Like with vfx, this will influence technical and team structure needs.

UNDERSTANDING THE AUDIO VISION

In terms of tone and experiential feedback, few of the visions are as powerful as the audio vision. Audio is able to carry, connect and subvert emotion and expectations in powerful ways. Which means understanding the vision and intent being defined by the Head of Audio is incredibly valuable and important. Audio and animation go hand in hand and equally rely upon one another to bring about believable and reactive characters and worlds.

Music

While the music is unlikely to directly impact animation, it is certainly one of the most impactful components of tone and emotion. Understanding the genre and style of music will give you a deep well to draw from in terms of research and reference when needing to convey or stay in a consistent mood. This will also allow you to know where music is intended to be doing the emotional heavy lifting and where it will be the glue that connects transitions between scenes and features. If you start gathering appropriate music selections now, it will make your job around Communicating the Vision easier, as discussed in Chapter 8.

Voice

Acting is comprised of voice and actions, so understanding the vision and direction behind vocal performances is incredibly important in terms of creating consistent character performances. You will want to understand who is going to be directing vocal performances and what their intended direction is. Some good questions to ask the Head of Audio are:

- *Who is directing vocal performances?*

- *What is the intended style and tone of the vocal performance?*

- *What is the casting process for vocal performers?*

- *What is the recording process?*

All of this is an effort to align a character's performance across all aspects of the game and build the foundation for consistency and support across all elements of capture and realization. Start having conversations early about actor contracts and the need to capture face, voice and body, as well as how and when that can happen. The more you can capture at once, the more consistent and of higher quality the full realization of the performance will be.

Localization

Localization is all about how the game is planned to be translated and adapted to different regions and cultures. This can impact animation support in terms of voice acting and content ratings. Will characters need lip sync to match each recorded language, or will other languages be dubbed and/or subtitled? Are there certain actions or behaviors that are insensitive in different regions of the world? While it might sound like there will be a need to make new animations to support this, in most cases, when it comes to these needs, the solutions are often technical-focused. And more often than not, the sooner these needs are identified, the solutions can be rather trivial extensions of your existing workflows. But you will definitely want to take these localization needs into account when Defining Technical Needs in Chapter 4.

Once you have done the above deep dives across all of the disciplines, you are likely to feel both overwhelmed and inspired by the amount of information you now have. You will clearly see some consistent trends across all of the visions, which should give you for the first time a bird's-eye view of the entire project. It is at this point that it can be tempting to jump right into defining the animation vision of the game, and you should definitely start taking some notes and writing down ideas throughout this process. But before you focus on defining the animation vision for what you think is the game, it is important to open up your creative toolbox and examine the tools that are inside.

NOTES

1 Steve Swink's *Game Feel: A Game Designer's Guide to Virtual Sensation* (2008) should be part of every game animator's library, the same way so many animation craft books are. The way it presents the overlap of all disciplines to create actions with intent has been instrumental in how I continue to think and talk about gameplay and animation systems.

2 While everyone thinks they can write (I type, as I write a book), it would be foolish to believe we know the depth of any craft we are not dedicated to. Luckily, thanks to the very nature of narrative, often starting with the written word, there is no shortage of books on the topic. I would specifically recommend Hannah Nicklin's *Writing for Games: Theory and Practice* (2022) as a great place to start. She comes from a theater background, which has obvious overlaps with animation, and she does a wonderful job of diving into how it relates to games.

3 Cinematography is an area in which I am not as well versed as gameplay, but whenever I need a refresher, I turn to Steve Katz's *Film Directing Shot by Shot: Visualizing from Concept to Screen* (1991) and Joseph Mascelli's *Five C's of Cinematography* (1965).

4 I would be remise not to mention my love for Ed Hooks. His enthusiasm and willingness to engage in all things acting and animation have been transformative in how I think about interactive animation. A lot of Chapter 6 is informed by conversations I have had with Ed and the various books and readings he has recommended. If you do not already own a copy, you should immediately purchase *Acting for Animators*.

CHAPTER 3

Defining the Tools and Craft

W HERE THE FIRST COUPLE of chapters have been more focused on listening to the head, this chapter will start to touch on topics near and dear to the heart and gut of animation, which means it is time to talk about art and the creative process. And while this section is specifically going to focus on the tools available to create animation, I want to start with my definition of art, as that will certainly give you insight into how I approach and think about the creative process.

The best definition of art I have come to accept is:

Art is communicating an idea with creative intent.

And the word *intent* is doing a lot of the heavy lifting in that sentence, as I like to illustrate with the example of stop signs. Stop signs are manufactured every day by a combination of people using tools and machines to ultimately create something that is designed to communicate a specific message. STOP! Is each stop sign you come across in the world a piece of art, though? I believe most people would say no. And that is because each individual stop sign in the world lacks creative *intent*.

In contrast, if you were to show people the original concept design of a stop sign, a compelling photograph of a stop sign, or if someone were to hand craft a stop sign out of glass, most people would consider those to be works of art. The reason is that there is a clear creative *intent* of an

 DOI: 10.1201/9781003356196-3

individual being communicated in each of these pieces. Where this discussion can become a bit more divisive is if someone were to pull a stop sign from the ground and hang it in a gallery. In this case, creative intent is again being applied, similar to that of a photograph. But the contention point in this case is more likely to be around if the art is 'good' or 'successful.' And what defines that success is the *encounter* between the creation and the person engaging with it.

I italicize *encounter* as it is a term that comes from the psychologist Rollo May in his book *The Courage to Create*.[1] While he uses *encounter* to mean how the artist engages with the subject of their creation, I also like to think of the *encounter* as something that happens between the person engaging with the artist's work. Because how each person engages with it, especially in a medium as interactive as games, ultimately defines the success of the creative intent being communicated. And for us, as interactive animators, we have many people engaging across the development team and the people that experience the final creation.

That is to say, the investigations of the previous chapter that went into informing the intent of the project and the entire development team will allow us to fully commit to what we will need to create, which means it is now time to talk about the tools of creation.

EFFORT AND VALUE

With the above definition of art, the reliance on intent and the awareness of the encounter, the tools used in the creation of the work are not a defining factor of what makes something inherently artistic. The tools play a role in how the artist is able to communicate their idea, and their comfort with those tools will indeed influence how successful they are in communicating as closely as possible what they intend. But no tool is inherently more artistic than another. Because one tool requires more effort than another, that does not make it more valuable. Effort is purposefully not included in the above definition of art or what makes it successful, for good reason.

Since almost the beginning of animation, there has been a tension between the craft of the artist and the production methods by which animation can be created.[2] Artists like Windsor McKay would actively promote the number of drawings and the intense singular effort that went into their films as a key point towards proving their creative value. This was directly meant to contrast the films being made by production companies employing multiple people and techniques to produce films more quickly (Figure 3.1).

FIGURE 3.1   A still from *Little Nemo* (1911) showing Windsor McKay in a dramatized animation studio.

Decades later, you can see a clear through line from that to Pixar promoting the use of 'No motion capture or any other performance shortcuts' at the end of *Ratatouille*. This instills a belief in those watching, learning and creating animation that effort is a key ingredient in how art derives its value. Or, in other terms, what makes the art successful. And while often this is being done as an act of defiance against those that look to extract and maximize value from the artists or by students dedicating themselves to learning a new craft, by actively assigning value to effort, we allow ourselves to have our passion be exploited by those looking to profit from it.

This is not to say the work required to execute a creative vision does not require effort. It certainly does, and new ideas or approaches can be especially challenging. There is also something to be said about creative intent and mastery of the craft coming from the often discussed 10,000 hours dedicated to learning a skill. And the tedium of traditional practices can create some necessary friction and flow in the creative process, which forces the mind to switch between conscious and unconscious modes of thinking. It also requires a fuller understanding and appreciation of how something is made, which can be lost as new technology obscures some of the necessary workings.[3]

But it is important to remember that in a collaborative creative endeavor, as this book is focused on, the entire team is best served if you work smarter, not harder, as the often-repeated saying goes. Every tool is best suited for specific actions and crafting specific creations. Yes, you can use a singular tool to create almost anything, but it is important to be honest and ask yourself why you are not using every tool available to you. If you are adding a level of difficulty by dismissing a valuable tool for the explicit sake of celebrating the effort required by using another, you are doing your entire team a disservice.

All of this is to say that the tension between art and production is not inherently something to be reviled. Tension, friction and constraints, when applied with intent, are fantastic motivators for creativity. They can drive the natural back and forth between the conscious and unconscious thought processes, creating 'A HA!' moments that ultimately unlock new creative ideas and opportunities. And when those new creative ideas and opportunities arise, being comfortable using all of the tools in your toolbox and knowing which can provide the right amount of tension to allow for 'A HA!' moments will allow you to execute on a powerful and personal creative vision. So let's look at the benefits of the different types of tools available and how best to take them into account with a creative vision.

KEYFRAME

Keyframe animation is easily the most flexible of the animation options available for any project. No matter the art style, the tech or the team, keyframe is always available. The only real constraint with a keyframe is time. With enough time, you can achieve any style or reach any level of quality. You can always invest more time into training the team to strengthen their keyframe skills. It is possible to add more joints, controls, blend shapes or shaders to allow for the ability to better control the pose, expression and form of a character. With time, all things are possible.

That catch, of course, is that time is a variable constraint. And when it comes to a commercial project, time, like everything else, equates to money. More time comes at the cost of extending the deadline or adding more people. And ironically enough, to do either of these is often the most time-consuming process to make happen. So unless you have unlimited time and money, there are two incredibly important things to focus on when relying on keyframe animation. Frictionless workflows and scope control.

If keyframe animation is at the core of your project, it will mean you still want to take this into account in the next chapter focused on technical needs. Specifically, you will want to highlight workflows that slow down the team, with long iteration loops or areas of specific friction, such as opening or saving files with multiple characters. Frictionless workflows should always be a priority, but especially so when time is the only hurdle to overcome. Shaving seconds or minutes off of common work flows is literally giving everyone on the team more time.

The other area to focus on is scope control, which will be covered in depth in Chapter 10. Knowing how to make the most of each animation and where best to focus the time spent is absolutely key to making the most of your keyframes.

CAPTURE

Capture, be it motion capture, facial capture or combined as part of performance capture, is a powerful tool available in the animation toolbox. The ability to work with experts in different styles of motion and acting to capture movement and performances on a large scale is not something to ever dismiss. Some of my favorite time spent on any project is on the capture stage, working with people who have talent, skills and expertise that is both inspiring and humbling. However, there can be a lot of strong feelings for or against the inclusion of capture. And it is important to honestly engage with those feelings to understand the concerns or frustrations the team is likely to experience. And it generally manifests in a few ways.

The first is around the myth of effort defining the value of the craft. As described above, this is something baked into the core of how animation has always been valued and marketed. But beyond that, effort and value have a long history of being tangled up and exploited through education, belief systems and cultural norms. That is to say, this is not something you should expect to be able to address in a single conversation. But what you can focus on in terms of this concern are the areas where they put effort into the craft that they enjoy or fear losing out on. This will help you to understand what they creatively value in their work, which you can then both find space for, as well as highlight the opportunity for capture to further advance. All of which often leads to the next concern.

Another common concern is losing a sense of creative intent or a specific execution of the craft. This often comes from the public perception of capture, which is that the actors are marketed as those with the creative intent driving a character's performance. This has led to anima-tors being ignored[4] or even under-valued[5] in the capture process. And this can often be born out of animators being handed capture data in bulk with little to no input or even context given. And the larger the project and the tighter the deadline, this can be an easy situation to fall into. For people on the team that directly voice a concern in this aspect, it is important to make space for their involvement in the capture pro-cess. It could be getting into the motion capture suits themselves to pro-totype and appreciate the craft[6] of the actors involved in capture. Giving every team member the opportunity to direct actors on the stage cer-tainly allows them to transfer their knowledge of the character and fea-tures directly to the actor giving the performance. Or even having team members on the floor or watching remotely on a call with the ability to give notes to the director can all empower engagement and enthusiasm around the collaborative process that capture affords.

A similar concern is that capture will replace the need for animators. Some of this comes from the same public perception around how cap-ture is marketed, and some of this comes from the regularly increasing quality of raw capture data. But just like 3d animation hasn't replaced 2d animation and the camera didn't replace painting, this is a concern that hasn't come true. It has indeed changed the nature of many animation jobs. Again, it is a tool, and as tools go, it is a pretty handy one that can be used in a number of ways. But there will always be characters and actions that cannot be captured. And even for those that can be captured, that is not the end of the animation process, as editing will need to happen, and that always benefits from an animator's sensibilities.

Which leads to the final big misconception around capture, which is that the raw capture data is plug-and-play out of the box. This impression is gener-ally accompanied by the expectation that capture will immediately increase the animation team's output and even quality. While it is very true that cap-ture can help speed up the process of creating new animation data, the raw data being 100% ready to use on delivery is very much a rare exception, not the rule. And to even get to the point that the exception can ever happen, there is a lot of care that is required in creating quality-solving and retar-geting pipelines. So more often than not, the captured data will require an animator's attention, from retiming the performance to pushing poses and even splicing together different takes and actions to meet the requirements of a feature or scene. It is better to think of capture getting you 50%–75%

of the way. The more attention paid to the craft and quality of the capture pipeline, the closer you can get to 80%. The less attention paid to the capture pipeline, the closer you can get to 10%–20%. When talking to people outside of animation who want to leverage capture, it is important to convey that it is a long-term investment, not an immediate solution. And the more you invest in the process, the more you will get out of it.

In terms of style and tone, capture is almost as flexible as a keyframe. Yes, it starts from a more realistic place, but even reality can be more fantastic than we give it credit for. From performers trained in all manner of movement, the human body can do some pretty incredible things. When you add wire work, spring boards and other on-set modifications, not to mention the ability for animators to further edit the captured data after the fact, capture can be applied at a foundational level to almost any style or tone.

PROCEDURAL

I am using the term procedural here to cover several movement and performance generation methods. Or, to cite Daniel Holden,[7] another term to classify this section would be indirect control methods. This would be tools like powered Ragdoll,[8] procedural interpolation,[9] motion matching,[10] machine learning[11] and IK layering.[12] This is work that largely happens at runtime, in the engine. But this would also include simulations or constraint systems within a dcc package.[13] This is an ever-advancing area of research and application. I am sure whatever I write now will already be dated by the time you read it. Which is why, instead of speaking to the specifics on any of these, I want to focus more on how to approach these methods and general tech advancements and paradigm shifts in relation to animation vision, style and tone.

If you plan on relying on these methods, it is often best to think about how they can be used in bulk across as many parts of the game as possible. Either as the core component of your systems, so that it gets the appropriate focus and support required to pull it off. Or as something you can add to existing components to layer in additional reactivity. When it comes to new technologies, workflows and approaches, there are usually two tipping points.

The first is when you are using proprietary or early adoption of new technology. Generally, the workflows and the ability to influence, polish and adjust for desired results are works in progress. So in order to get the most out of the tool or approach, it needs to be able to be applied to a level that offsets the effort that would have gone into creating the directly controlled, individual animations if done in a more traditional, established manner. For instance, when working on Agents of Mayhem, we had a procedural IK system that we could additively apply to any character in the game. This meant hit reactions, jump lands and jog-to-sprint transitions could be created entirely in the engine. While the method of creating each of those the first time was more intensive than if we had animated them in maya, the fact that we could apply it across every character once created meant that we had a one-and-done solution. Across enough characters, the investment was well worth it, as any polishing or tuning of each would benefit the look and feel across every character in the game.

The other tipping point is when one of these indirect control methods becomes adopted by enough people in the industry that even when adopting it for the first time on your team, answers and best approaches will exist to show the benefits and weaknesses of each approach. I am proud to say that the game animation industry has grown into one that openly shares its best practices and technology. To not directly engage with the knowledge being shared is a disservice to yourself and your team.

At this point, it feels like we are now listening more to the head than to the heart and gut, but understanding the output and results of these indirect, procedural methods of animation will inform your heart and gut about several new creative opportunities. Because when approached in that way, the results can produce a style and tone entirely unique and delightful.[14] And at the very least, it can allow for some amusing Easter eggs.[15]

None of these tools should be seen as zero sums. All of the projects I have worked on over the last 10 years have used all of these in some combination, for both the body and face. But like any tool, it first needs to exist, and once used, it needs to be taken care of and maintained, which leads us into our next chapter focused on technical needs.

NOTES

1 Rollo May's *The Courage to Create* (1975) is a psychoanalytic look at the creative process. While I cite his use of *encounter* here, he also discusses the idea of creativity and "A HA!" moments living in the transition between the conscious and unconscious mind, which I also touch on in this chapter.

2 While I specifically cite Nicholas Sammond's *Birth of an Industry: Blackface Minstrelsy and the Rise of American Animation* (2015) in terms of how animation, production and labor have been almost immediately in tension with one another, as the title states, the book is about a lot more than that.

It is a thorough and well-researched history of the American animation industry that will show without a doubt how much racism has been baked into the visual language of animation.

3 I only touch on it briefly here, but Matthew Crawford's *Shop Class as Soulcraft: An Inquiry into the Value of Work* (2010) does a great job breaking down the history of, as well as his own personal experience, how trades and crafts have been looked down upon for generations as less than white collar, managerial or business-focused work. And how technology has obscured a lot of the still necessary trade work, making maintenance and the understanding of how things work more of a need now than ever before. This can be paired well with Catherine Liu's *Virtue Hoarders: The Case against the Professional Managerial Class* (2021) and Barbara Ehrenreich's *Fear of Falling: The Inner Life of the Middle Class* (2020) to look at the other side of how the focus on managerial work has set people up for failure. All of which further demonstrates the need to focus on intent, not effort, as where the best way to assign value to artistic creations. Or said in another way, by Erik Hoel in his post *AI Art isn't Art* (2022) "...rather than talking about the 'mechanical production' of art, in our new age we must be concerned with the 'non-conscious production' of art."

4 During the marketing of almost any game, you are likely to see the focus on the actor more than the rest of the team that brought a character to life. A perfect example is this 2022 Game Informer article titled *God of War Ragnorak's Director Fought to Keep Its Most Unexpected and Cartoonish Character*. Even if it isn't malicious, it is clear how poor crediting practices and the cult of personality around specific roles, despite an inherently collaborative creation, have allowed for a character's performance to be turned into a marketing beat that regularly leaves out certain people. This is not to dismiss those who are celebrated. One of my favorite parts of games is the cross-discipline collaboration required to realize anything. But we need to be better about not attributing the majority of the success to upstream roles by erasing those downstream.

5 An example of something that does feel more malicious and dismissive of a team's effort is well covered in this 2014 Cinemablend article *Andy Serkis Calls Motion Capture 'Digital Makeup', Riles Up Animators*.

6 Performing for *Motion Capture: A Guide for Practitioners* (2022) by John Dower and Pascal Langdale is a fantastic read for anyone putting on a suit or directing capture for the first time. It gives a great overview on the specific needs of acting for a capture space, as well as some foundations for different acting theories and approaches.

7 Daniel Holden's 2022 *SCA 2022 – Keynote by Daniel Holden: Future Animation Systems* gives a great overview of the state of animation technology, released as I was writing part of this book. I also appreciate his terminology in terms of direct and indirect control and how to think about the way people engage in the creative process.

8 Michael Mach's *Physics Animation in Uncharted 4: A Thief's End* 2017 GDC talk gives a wonderful breakdown on how to apply Ragdoll to different scenarios.

9 David Rosen's 2014 talk *An Indie Approach to Procedural Animation* rocked the animation community's mind when he presented it and you can see his approach influencing multiple games, engines and tools. His approach of using a handful of poses and entirely procedural motion is a powerful 'A HA!' moment for anyone used to working with more traditional methods.

10 There are a number of talks that describe how to approach motion matching, but Kristjan Zadziuk's *Motion Matching, The Future of Games Animation... Today* from 2016 is a great place to start in understanding the possibility space.

11 Almost anything I link here in regards to machine learning is destined to be out of date when this is published. But it is always a good idea to keep an eye on the work of Sebastian Starke. *[SIGGRAPH 2020] Sebastian Starke – Thesis Fast Forward* is a 2020 talk he gave, which shows a number of advancements he was a part of.

12 While it can be a bit reductive to say IK layering, beyond the procedural work outlined in David Rosen's talk, there is a lot of IK work that can work alongside traditionally created animation. A good example of how this can be applied is Alexander Bereznyak's 2016 talk, *IK Rig: Procedural Pose Animation*.

13 While everything linked up to this point has been runtime or engine-focused, it can very much exist within software outside of engines. Cascadeur is one example, as outlined in this 2019 talk *Cascadeur: Physics-Based Animation Manifest* by Evgeniy Dyabin and Alexander Grishanin.

14 Animation style will be discussed more in depth in Chapter 7, but for some great examples of leaning into procedural tech as a style, you should watch *Huddle Up! Making the [SPOILER] of INSIDE* by the team at Playdead and *The Rain World Animation Process* by Joar Jacobsson and James Therrien. The care and application of the craft result in truly charming and surprising results.

15 What started as a bug in our procedural system on *Agents of Mayhem* (the land 'animation' would endlessly loop once triggered) was turned into my favorite Easter egg I have been a part of, as you can see in the *1930s Cartoon Mode Easter Egg! Agents of Mayhem* youtube video.

CHAPTER 4

Defining Technical Needs

ALL OF THE BEST design, narrative, art and animation visions will fall flat if the project doesn't have the technical and engineering support required to bring it to life. When it comes to other mediums that employ animation, the problem of 'how do we make the character move on the screen?' is largely solved. Which allows the animation team to largely focus on 'why is the character moving at all?' And when they talk about a character's performance, it is in terms of acting choices. But for games, performance can just as much mean how well the character actually functions in the game from a technical standpoint.

Animation technology is a rapidly growing and evolving field. Keeping up with advancements can be a fulltime job, and while the technology is becoming more and more animator-friendly, it just as quickly becomes more complex in new ways. Few people are able to have a firm grasp of the craft of animation and the deep technical knowledge required to realize all of it in games. In my specific case, I know just enough about current and future technology to be dangerous. Which is why I employ due diligence early on in a project to make sure the technical requirements needed to support animation are well understood and documented. This starts by taking all of the previous discipline visions and creating a clear vision of what is being requested by animation. Some people like to make target game footage[1] to prove this. I however prefer cutting together a

DOI: 10.1201/9781003356196-4

competitive analysis video at this stage. And use target game footage as part of the vision videos in Chapter 8.

COMPETITIVE ANALYSIS VIDEO

This video, also known as a rip-o-matic, is essentially a montage of clips from other games, focused on the features of the project and how they have been realized by others in the space. This is not meant to convey tone or style, as that will come later. The goal of this video is to demonstrate what will be required of animation to support the vision of the project. Creating this video will be key to not only the technical needs of this chapter but also Defining Team Structure in Chapter 5 and Communicating the Vision in Chapter 8. As an example of this, I am including the Gameplay Animation Analysis video[2] I made during early pre-production on *Dragon Age* (Figure 4.1).

This was one of two competitive analysis videos I made for the project. The other was focused on cinematic and facial animation. This essentially meant one video focused on gameplay and action, the other on narrative and acting. Depending on the breadth and scale of the project, having multiple videos can be valuable, as you want to be able to accurately convey the needs of each feature.

For this gameplay analysis video, I identified the following areas of the player experience as important based on the cross-discipline vision investigations:

FIGURE 4.1   A screen shot from Jonathan Colin's *Horizon Zero Dawn* Game Animation Reel showing Aloy scrambling up a hill. Copyright Sony.

- *Traversal*
    - *Reactive Player Traversal*
    - *Frictionless Traversal*
    - *Scripted Traversal*

- *World Reactivity*
    - *Appropriate and Fast Interactions*
    - *Player Contextual Transitions*
    - *Environmental Animation*
    - *AI Awareness*

- *Combat*
    - *Team Combat*
    - *Fast-Synced Kills*
    - *Signature-Synced Kills*
    - *AI-Driven Syncs*
    - *Environmental Syncs*
    - *Multicharacter Syncs*

- *Epic Scale Fights*

As an action RPG, the core part of gameplay was to revolve around traversal, world reactivity and combat, more so than in previous titles. This made it important to showcase specific examples of the different elements as discussed and referenced by project visions and needs. It is especially important to include elements that the team hasn't made before to help establish shared expectations on how those elements will be realized.

The hope is that as each feature comes online, you could replace the clips in this video with ones from the game you are making. Which means, if you were to squint hard enough, this is one of the first opportunities you all have to see how the game should come together. And to ask yourself and the rest of the project leadership if this looks like the game you are all intending to make. Because if anything in this video seems off, now is the perfect time to remove or replace that clip with something that is more representative of the project vision.

Edit requests like that can lead to the inclusion of a clip like that at the 1:06 mark. That was highlighted as *Too Appropriate and Slow* as an example of an antivision. This was included to set expectations and assuage concerns from other discipline directors around the desire to have interaction animations that felt attached to the world but didn't take away control from the player for too long. More on this can be found in Chapter 8, around communicating a vision. While we are on that topic, and at the risk of diverging too much into what we will cover in that chapter, there are a couple of important points to keep in mind when cutting together this video.

While this video is meant to speak more to the function than the form, it is impossible to entirely divorce those two things. By using other video games as references, there are likely common tropes or actions that may be on display that will not match the actual tone or vision of the game. To that end, there are a few conscious creative choices employed in this video to try to control those expectations. The first is to include a sound track that does not directly match what is expected of the game. This is as much a tech demo as a realization of the presentation. Your music choice can influence and drive that perception. The other creative choice here was to include a clip at the end that does start to speak to tone. Like when making a demo reel, you want to end on a high note, as that is what will stick with the viewer after they finish watching. Including the Epic Scale Fight helps to wrap up everything seen with a slight aftertaste of the intended tone and fantasy of the gameplay experience.

I also try to treat vision videos like demo reels. Any video over 2 minutes long runs the risk of having people lose attention. So only include the most important and best representative clips required. We will further cover how best to communicate a vision to different audiences in Chapter 8, but in this case, because the core audience is both project leadership and technical experts, the time range can run a little longer since this is incredibly relevant information to define and then dissect.

Spending the time to make this a video that people, especially project leadership, will want to engage with is important. That will help them align with and agree with what is highlighted in this video. Which will then allow you to move forward with confidence in defining the tech needs required to pull it off.

ANALYSIS VIDEO BREAKDOWN

Now that we have a video demonstrating the needs of animation on the project, we can start breaking down each video clip piece by piece in terms of the technology and disciplines required to support all of it. This is going to require conversations with a number of discipline experts, so you will want to go into those conversations with a clear plan.

The first step is to create a document that details what is needed in each clip in terms of technology and people. The format of the document can be set up in a rather straightforward way to make sure there is consistency in how each clip is discussed and defined. What you need is:

- *Area of Focus*
  - *Specific needs displayed in the clip (timestamp of clip in the video)*
    - *New tech required to support the feature*
    - *Existing tech that can be leveraged*
    - *The people needed to support the feature*

Looking back to the first couple of clips in the gameplay competitive analysis video, the first showing Alloy from *Horizon: Zero Dawn* running up and down the slopes and the second showing Arthur Morgan from *Red Dead Redemption II* walking through the snow, you can see how the entire document would look.

- *Reactive Player Traversal*
  - *Running up and down slopes triggers new animations (0:04–0:15)*
    - *New Tech Required*
    - *Builds on Existing Tech*
    - *Staff Required to Implement*
  - *Moving through Snow, Water, Mud, etc. (0:15–0:19)*
    - *New Tech Required*
    - *Builds on Existing Tech*
    - *Staff Required to Implement*

Once you have done this for every clip, you are now prepared to detail the specific needs required to support everything in the video. Anything you know the answer to can, of course, be filled out. But the main purpose of this is to sit down with the discipline experts to go over the video and fill it out together. There can be a number of assumptions that are either out of date or misunderstood when it comes to technical capabilities, no matter how long people have used a specific set of tools. This is the perfect opportunity to get everyone on the same page about the needs of the project and what is required to support it.

I prefer to run through this individually with each member of the animation tech team, depending on the size of the team. This gives a fresh perspective to each problem, allows you to assess the strengths and areas of interest for each person, gives them an early chance to feel included in the process and makes sure each person's voice is heard. The point of these investigations is to not only understand the technical needs but also the expertise and capabilities of your team. It can be easy to always rely on one or two people as the tech experts, but this can be a good opportunity to spread the knowledge and opportunities to others.

After talking through each clip with discipline experts, you are likely to find your breakdowns look something like this.

- *Reactive Player Traversal*
    - *Running up and down slopes triggers new animations (0:04–0:15)*
        - *New Tech Required*
            - *Need ground slope angle exposed to animation systems*
            - *Future physics predictive path generation*
            - *Physics/Collision Capsule support*
        - *Builds on Existing Tech*
            - *Animation Systems*
                - *Motion Matching for new movement sets*
                - *Procedural ground IK for adjustments to sets*
                - *Slope adjust for foot/hand IK & warping*

- *Game Systems*

  o *Slope plane tracked here*

- *Staff Required to Implement*

  - *Animator for Assets, Anim Systems work, Ground IK tweaks*

  - *Technical Animator for Slope and Ground IK setup*

  - *Programmer for exposing/feeding slope data to Anim Systems*

  - *Level Designer for defining/maintaining slope metrics*

- *Moving through Snow, Water, Mud, etc. (0:15–0:19)*

  - *New Tech Required*

    - *Data Hooks for World Markup*

    - *Shader work for Terrain Deformation*

  - *Builds on Existing Tech*

    - *Animation Systems*

      o *Motion Matching and Context Databases for new movement sets*

    - *Game Systems*

      o *Material Editor support*

      o *Shader Terrain Deformation*

  - *Staff Required to Implement*

    - *Animator for Animations & Motion Matching work*

    - *Programmer for Material Editor hooks*

    - *Level Designer for world markup*

    - *Gameplay Designer for speed & feel of locomotion*

    - *Tech/Shader Artist for Terrain Deformation*

As you can see, this quickly adds up to a lot of work and disciplines required. It can almost be overwhelming when you look at it in full. But you can already see in these two examples some consistent threads of work that will be needed in specific areas. And you will now specifically be better informed of the different tech and workflows that exist. Which now allows you to break down each of the tech needs into a few different areas with more confidence. When it comes to who is responsible for any area of animation tech, it can be a bit confusing. I am including here the areas of influence, type of work and roles generally associated with the work required to help give some framework on how to classify the above findings.

Technical Animation Needs

This is easily the most unclear title and set of responsibilities that exist within animation. And maybe game development teams as a whole. This can include people who do everything from rigging and skinning to setting up complex runtime behaviors. But for the sake of clarifying responsibilities, I like to use the two sides of the animation tech needs as a razor. DCC technical needs would be defined as work done in software packages like Maya, MotionBuilder, Blender, etc. And runtime technical needs, which happen in the engine. As an additional complication, there can also be confusion about the runtime needs between character setup and deformation work versus systems and behavior work. While that isn't as clear a division, when I talk about technical animation or technical animators, I specifically mean the character setup and deformation work. And I break out the system's work into its own category. Looking at technical animation in this way gives space and preference to a more traditional definition of the role when it first evolved, before engines allowed for more complex animation systems work to be done by disciplines outside of programming.

Examples of the specific animation tech work I would attribute to technical animators are as follows:

- *DCC*
    - *Rigging*
    - *Skinning*
    - *Tools*
    - *Pipelines*
    - *Retargeting*

- *Runtime*
  - *Character Setup*
  - *IK*
  - *Cloth*
  - *Ragdoll*
  - *Shaders*
  - *Retargeting*

Viewing the specific needs through this lens will help to quickly clarify the specific sort of skillset and expertise you need to support this work. As mentioned, the runtime responsibilities can become a bit unclear around who does that work as it pushes outside of explicit character deformation. Which is why we have the next group.

Animation System Needs

Animation system designers are one of the newer specific skillsets to have evolved within the animation space. This is a group of people that are focused on how the animations play and operate at runtime. They spend their time almost exclusively in engine, focused on the systems and logic that string and layer together animations. Generally, as this is a newer skillset for people to be focused on, you will find a mix of animators, technical animators and designers doing this sort of work. And as animation tools and workflows in engines become more powerful, the need to have people specifically focused on this work can be important to help unify and optimize the systems driving animation across the game.

Examples of the specific animation tech work I would attribute to animation system designers are as follows:

- *State Machines*
- *Blend Spaces*
- *Runtime Layers*
- *Character Interactions*
- *Procedural Animation*
- *Motion Matching Setup*

There are a number of factors that will influence whether you need dedicated roles to handle this or if it can be shared across disciplines. How technically inclined are your animators? How user-friendly and well-documented are the engine tools? How complex and interconnected are your animation systems? How many characters do you have in your game? How much of an existing foundation do you already have established for your runtime animation systems? The answers to all of that will dictate who should be doing this work, which we will get into more in the next chapter. But the value of having people who are systems-minded and focused on smoother implementation is a force multiplier for any animation team. So having this work specifically classified as its own section, regardless of who does the work, is important.

Animation Programming Needs

Programmers that are focused on animation support are one of the most difficult people to find. And having programmers entirely dedicated to animation is not a given at many studios. Often, animation programming support is shared by a mix of programmers across gameplay, AI, narrative and rendering. Which can make it all the more important to establish the animation programming needs early so that they can be taken into account across multiple discipline needs. Those also happen to be good areas to specifically break down the programming areas of support needed, as even if you have dedicated animation programmers, they will need to collaborate with the programmers in those areas.

Examples of the areas in which you can break down programming tech needs would be:

- *Player Character*

- *AI*

- *Physics*

- *Narrative*

- *Rendering*

- *Optimization*

You should be able to classify most of the defined technical needs across technical animation, animation systems and animation programming. Once you have done a pass organizing those, it is good to check back in with the experts in each group to verify the specific responsibilities are clear and appropriately delegated. However, there are likely to be some additional needs that will exist specifically outside of the animation department that you will want to make sure those teams are aware of.

Other Discipline Needs

It should be no surprise that there will be cross-discipline support required to deliver on technical needs within animation. Game development is a collaborative effort across many disciplines. But because the support needed is driven by elements of the game as defined by other disciplines on the project, it should be an easy case to make for why animation needs their support to develop these specific tech needs. And in most cases, there will be some specific disciplines you are most likely going to be relying upon when it comes to tech support.

- *Technical Designers*

- *Technical Artists*

- *Level Designers*

- *Gameplay Designers*

- *Environment Artists*

- *Character Artists*

- *VFX Artists*

- *Audio Engineers*

Honestly, you could list any and every discipline here, as this list is likely to include the disciplines most connected to the defining features of your project that make it unique. Which, like in the case of shared programming support, makes it all the more important to raise the need for support early, as they are likely to have a full plate already.

The delegation of which discipline, person or group is responsible for any of the work around the required technical needs can vary per studio or project. If your team's roles and definitions vary from how I defined them, that is fine. As long as there is a consistent and shared understanding within your team and project, that is all that matters.

From this point forward, none of the vision videos will employ games as references. It has been valuable to reference other games in terms of functional needs and to engage with design and tech. But at this point, the creative vision and tech needs are well defined, and using other games to define your vision will at best come across as well-executed tropes. And at worst, a forgettable clone. There is an entire universe to draw inspiration from, which we will discuss in Chapter 6.

With this information, you should now have a clear understanding of the tech required to support the needs of the project. Which means you can now move onto defining your team structure in the next chapter, which, alongside the technical needs, should help you pitch to project leadership the animation team's needs.

NOTES

1 Beyond talking about target game footage in his book, Jonathan Cooper has some fantastic examples on his GameAnim website in a 2020 post titled *The Target Game Footage.*

2 You can see the video as part of the supplemental information available on the CRC Press website for this book. It is titled Video_CompetitiveAnalysis. mp4.

CHAPTER 5

Defining Team Structure

I T DOESN'T MATTER HOW great the vision or tech is for your project if you don't have the right team. Along with establishing a clear vision, building a strong and empowered team should be your top priority. There are a number of great books and resources[1] about leadership, but I am especially fond of how Donella Meadows described it in her book *Thinking in Systems*[2]:

> *"Hierarchical systems evolve from the bottom up. The purpose of the upper layers of the hierarchy is to serve the purposes of the lower layers."*

Through your conversations around expectations, project needs and tech requirements, you have been learning and defining the purpose of those lower layers. Which has naturally built foundation of trust and respect with your team. Which is great because, from the outset of a project, you will need to be thinking about how best to structure your team to grow and adapt to the different stages of the development process. That can feel overwhelming, with so many variables and unknowns early on in a project, but that is what we will be focused on in this chapter. And if you feel you are still not connecting with members of your team, there are a number of ways to engage and connect as part of Chapter 12.

TEAM SIZE CALCULATOR

Something people often focus on is their team size. Do you have enough people? Will you need more people? Do you have the right people? There is never a clear answer to those questions, as it will vary depending on the features,

DOI: 10.1201/9781003356196-5

tech, workflows, people and time you have available. And based on your tech needs, you should be able to start estimating your high-level scope and costs, which are discussed in Chapter 10. But figuring out accurate estimates and costs for all of that will take time, so in order to get a rough idea early on, I created the *Game Animation Team Size Calculator*.[3] You can use this sheet to better understand and quantify the different team sizes across the industry and how the team size you are leading relates to competitive titles. These numbers have been gathered from either team members directly reporting on their team size through the *Post Project Animation Team Survey*[4] or extracted from the credits.

There are a number of caveats to this list, so it is in no way a silver bullet when working with production or studio leadership in trying to validate solid team requests. More specifically, this is meant to get you in the ballpark by looking at industry trends and getting an idea of generally how many people you should expect to need per feature to reach the competitive quality bar your game is aiming for.

There are two tabs available. The *Verified Sheet* tab is what we will be focused on. It is locked to verify accuracy and keep edits from happening to the public sheet. The other tab, *Form Responses*, shows the responses from the survey, which are pulled over to the verified tab. We will discuss the value of that survey more as part of Chapter 12, so for our purposes now, we will focus on the first tab.

In the top row of the sheet, you can enter your current animation team information. Make sure to also fill out how many hours of cinematics are being estimated, if those are part of the project (Figure 5.1).

Next is setting the quality bar next to the games on the list that match the competitive quality bar you are aiming for in your game (Figure 5.2).

I have filled out the sheet as an example of what I could expect a AAA project to aim for as having a reasonable quality bar within the next year or two as of the time I wrote this. This does not mean that the games listed as *Below* have bad animation. In fact, all of these games have had their animation specifically called out as a strength of the game and experience. It just happens that some are either a bit older now or their systems aren't as complex to stack up to more recent technology. I have personally worked on two of the games I listed as *Below*, and I am still incredibly proud of the animation work within. But again, this is all rather subjective at a certain point, so definitely adjust these as you see fit to match your tastes and needs.

YOUR GAME'S INFORMATION	Quality Bar	Animation Leadership	Gameplay Animators	Cinematic Animators	Additional/OS Animators	Technical Animators (DCC)	Technical Animators (Systems)	Animation Programmers	Outsource/Managers	Dev Years	Cinematic Hours	Shared Features	Genre
Guardians of the Galaxy	On Par	10	17	12	13	9	12	2	0		4		
Hades	Outlier	0	1	0	0	0.5	2			1.5	0		Indie
Hitman 2	On Par	2	9		7	4							Action
Hitman 3	On Par	1	4	2		2							Action
Horizon: Zero Dawn	On Par	4	9	5	13	7	2	6	0	5	3		OpenWorld
Horizon: Forbidden West	Outlier	9	19	44	3	12					20		OpenWorld
Immortals Fenyx Rising	Below	8	20	20	7	7		19					OpenWorld
It Takes Two	On Par	2	6		16	1					2.25		Indie
Jedi: Fallen Order	On Par	1	11	2	10	4	1	2	1	3	1		Action
Just Cause 3	Below	1	5	1	3	1.5	0	2	1	4	1		OpenWorld
Just Cause 4	Below	1	7	1	2	2	1	2	1	3	1		OpenWorld
Kena: Bridge of Spirits	On Par	1	14	5	1	1		1			1.1		Action
Kingdome Come Deliverance	Below	2	5		1	1	1				2		RPG
Last of Us 2	Above	3	15	70	20					4			Adventure
Mafia 3	On Par	1	5		7	3	1	1	0	3.5	4.5		OpenWorld
Marvel's Avengers	On Par	6	31		79	16	2				2.25		Action
Monster Hunter World	On Par	1	17	6	45	2		2			3		Action
Moss	Outlier	1											Indie
New World	On Par	4	9		24	9	1	0.5					MMO
Ori & Will of the Wisps	Outlier	2	3	2	5	2				6			Indie
Plague Tale: Innocence	On Par	2	5	5	16						1.2		Adventure
Plague Tale: Requiem	On Par	4	6	7	33	6					2		Adventure
Quantum Break	Below	1	3		4						4		Adventure
Ratchet & Clank: Rift Apart	Above	18	32		24	5			0				Action
Red Dead Redemption 2	Outlier	33	262	56	135			20	88	5	20		OpenWorld
Resident Evil 2	On Par	1	18	15	4	2		3	0		3		Adventure
Saints Row (2022)	On Par	3	6		12	1		1	1		2		OpenWorld
Sea of Thieves	On Par	1	5		5	2	2	2					OpenWorld
Sekiro	On Par	3	7	6							0.75		Action
Shadow of Mordor	On Par	1	7	5	3	1			1	5	1.5		OpenWorld
Shadow of War	On Par	2	10	16	1				0	3	3		OpenWorld
Spider-man	Above	3	11	19		6		5	0	4	2.5		OpenWorld
Stray	On Par	2	3		7	1			3				Adventure
Tomb Raider (2013)	On Par	4	13		8	3							Action
Tomb Raider: Rise of	On Par	8	12	13	29	3							Action
Tomb Raider: Shadow of	On Par	7	25	12	16	4	1						Action
Uncharted 4	Above	4		50	12								Adventure
Watch Dogs 2	Outlier	11	23	15	9	3		1	0	3	2.75		OpenWorld
Watch Dogs Legion	Outlier	19	21	13	10	4		1	0		2		OpenWorld
Witcher 3	On Par	1	10	7		0.5	5	3	0	4	13		OpenWorld

FIGURE 5.1 A screenshot of the team size calculator sheet, depicting various games and the number of people and cinematic hours required.

	Quality Bar
Ghosts of Tsushima	On Par ▾
God of War	Above ▾
Godfall	Below ▾
Guardians of the Galaxy	On Par ▾
Hades	Outlier ▾
Hitman 2	On Par ▾
Hitman 3	On Par ▾
Horizon: Zero Dawn	On Par ▾
Horizon: Forbidden West	Outlier ▾
Immortals Fenyx Rising	Below ▾
It Takes Two	On Par ▾
Jedi: Fallen Order	On Par ▾
Just Cause 3	Below ▾
Just Cause 4	Below ▾
Kena: Bridge of Spirits	On Par ▾
Kingdom Come Deliverance	Below ▾
Last of Us 2	Above ▾
Mafia 3	Below ▾
Marvel's Avengers	On Par ▾
Monster Hunter World	On Par ▾
Moss	Outlier ▾

FIGURE 5.2 A screenshot of the team size calculator sheet, depicting various games and subjectively assigned quality bars assigned to each.

At this point, once you have filled out the *Quality Bar Column* column of each project to fit your needs, you will see the projected number of people needed for your project. I have included both the Mean and Median, as the accuracy of each can fluctuate depending on the titles being grouped together (Figure 5.3).

Below	Animation Leadership	Gameplay Animators	Cinematic Animators	Additional Animators	Technical Animators	Animation System Designers	Animation Programmers	Outsource/Managers	Dev Years	Cinematic Hours	Shared Features
Mean	2	8.2	3.4	2.4	2	0.8	0.8	0.5	2.5	2.7	0
Median	1	7	3	3	2.5	1	1	0.5	3.5	1.5	#NUM!

On Par	Animation Leadership	Gameplay Animators	Cinematic Animators	Additional Animators	Technical Animators	Animation System Designers	Animation Programmers	Outsource/Managers	Dev Years	Cinematic Hours	Shared Features
Mean	2.8	11.4	9.4	17.4	3.5	1	1.4	0.9	2.2	4	0
Median	2	10	5	18	2.5	4	2	0	5	3	#NUM!

Above	Animation Leadership	Gameplay Animators	Cinematic Animators	Additional Animators	Technical Animators	Animation System Designers	Animation Programmers	Outsource/Managers	Dev Years	Cinematic Hours	Shared Features
Mean	5.4	17	42.7	10.7	1.7	0	0.7	1	3.7	1.8	0
Median	4	16	50	16	5	#NUM!	2	1.5	4	2.7	#NUM!

FIGURE 5.3 A screenshot of the team size calculator sheet, depicting the mean and median values of all of the games in the sheet across the different quality bars.

Within the sheet are two areas focused on features: The *Shared Features* column and the *Your Features* section. First you will want to fill out the *Your Features* section, which you should know after your conversations around Project Needs. Examples of features would be combat, traversal, multiplayer, living world, world interactions, etc. The *Shared Features* column can then be filled out, based on the number of features your game has, that the listed title shares.

The features portion is inherently the most nebulous part of the sheet and not meant to be used as concrete examples of team needs. It is meant more to illustrate that quality and team size are very much linked, as the higher quality titles have more animation support per feature or cinematic.

Finally, at the bottom, you will see how many animators your team currently has allocated per feature and cinematic hour (Figure 5.4).

With all of this in place, you can now easily compare the difference between the *On Par* team sizes and your current team size to make a

Game Animators/Feature	Cine Animators/Hour
2	5.9
1.3	3

Game Animators/Feature	Cine Animators/Hour
4.4	9.9
3.6	9.6

Game Animators/Feature	Cine Animators/Hour
5.5	23.6
5.3	20.2

FIGURE 5.4 A screenshot of the team size calculator sheet, depicting the number of animators per feature and hour of cinematic.

ballpark estimate on your required team size to meet your projected quality bar. And as new games come out, you can easily add to this list.

One other part of this is the *Genre* column that you could use to sort games by. While there is nothing built into the sheet to populate any data by genre, it might be something you find valuable if you look to make additional comparisons.

But again, this is not something you should expect to be accepted as a universal truth or fact in regards to staffing and budget resources. There are likely a couple of caveats that I am sure your production partners and project leadership will bring up that this sheet cannot answer.

- You don't know how many of the reported people were on any project for any specific amount of time. These are likely the numbers at full production, though even then, additional credits are likely for people who weren't there during full production. And outsource partners were likely scaled to these peak numbers at different times.

- Technical Animation, Animation System Designers and Animation Programming are hard to get full clarity on in terms of the type of work they are doing and if they are fully dedicated to animation work the entire time.

These are valid points, and you will still need to do the accurate scope and estimates described in Chapter 10. But early on in a project, when you need to give project leadership some idea of the team size they should expect to staff to meet the defined project needs, this will very quickly let you know if you are all aligned on where you will need to build.

TEAM LEADERSHIP ORGANIZATION

Now that you have an understanding of the project needs and an estimate of the team size you will likely need to grow towards to support those needs, you should think about how you want to structure the team you are directing. This is crucial to define, as it establishes the foundation of trust, support and expertise needed to scale your team, grow their skillsets and remain flexible with project iterations. The way a team is organized directly influences the primary communication of team members, so it is important to be intentional about making sure your structure makes the most of that reality. There are a few ways to approach this.

Discipline Focus

This is looking at the specific skillsets of the different disciplines on your team and creating a structure to keep them together as a central, shared support group across multiple areas of the project and team. This works well when you have a specific skillset or expertise that benefits from regular communication. This is also useful when you have a team that is required to support multiple areas of the game, necessitating team size or the complexity of the support work.

It may be that the entire animation department is thought of in this way, with you as the single person in a leadership position. This can work well if the team size is a few people and the focus of the project is more breadth than depth in any one area. However, once you get depth in features and skillsets or grow beyond five to nine people, this is unlikely to scale well without some additional leadership roles on the team.

Technical Animators/Artists or Animation Programmers are often the first to have the specific expertise and requirement of cross-feature support, so creating a discipline-focused leadership role specifically for these disciplines makes natural sense. Roles and responsibilities around animation tech are always evolving, as work in dcc packages like Maya, MotionBuilder or Blender overlaps with work being done in engines, so having this group connected allows for sharing of best practices and specific expertise (Figure 5.5).

Other examples of a discipline-focused approach can be for facial animation or motion capture, as both can be complex and focused endeavors that require dedicated expertise to support.

The benefits of this approach are that it keeps all of the craft experts together, which naturally leverages focused communication to drive a focus on craft quality. The downside of this approach is that it can silo the disciplines, negatively impacting their ability to regularly communicate with other disciplines on the project.

Area of Project Focus

Another approach is to look at how the project is being structured and embed the team into cross discipline focused areas or features. Think of groups like gameplay, cinematics, missions and world. This works

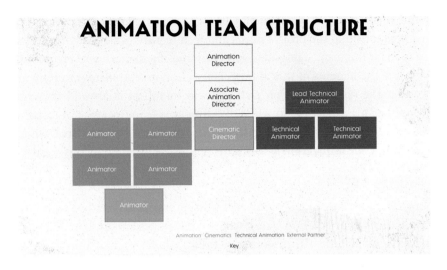

FIGURE 5.5   An example of a more discipline-focused team structure used at Compulsion Games on *South of Midnight*.

well when you need multiple disciplines and skillsets to collaborate and require constant communication. These can be smaller strike teams of a few people that move from feature to feature. Or it could be that the depth of experience or quantity of work requires a dedicated group to focus together on a specific area of the project. Another benefit of this approach is when you need to grow cross-discipline workflows and expertise in a team that hasn't done the specific work before.

As an example, when joining the *Dragon Age* team, it became clear early in pre-production that there was a need for animation support and narrative realization that did not fit neatly into gameplay or cinematics. It was the sort of in-world elements like ambient NPC life, scripted events and object interactions that in past games could fall through the cracks, with either gameplay or cinematics pitching in however they could towards the end of the project. This meant that the workflows for these sorts of elements were not well defined or tracked. And the cross-discipline communication with level artists, level designers and mission designers was lacking. Which can lead to a crunch to support or a less than stellar player experience if cut or hacked together.

The answer was to create a world animation team, pulling in team members from the gameplay and cinematic teams, to build the workflows and communication foundations required to support the needs of the game.

While this was a new department and focus for animation at BioWare, the investigations into the project needs and tech requirements easily identified the need for this team, alongside a gameplay and cinematics team (Figure 5.6).

While the benefits of this approach are clear, it is important to remember that the communication pull of team members is around the core group they are a part of. So when dividing up a team by areas of focus, it can make each animation group feel tighter connected to their area, which can mean communication across a discipline can become inconsistent.

Management Focus

No matter how a team is structured, by discipline, focus or some combination of the two, at a certain size, it will become important to share management responsibilities. This work generally includes regular one-on-ones, quarterly or annual reviews, mentorship, assisting with career growth, assigning and prioritizing task work or triaging bugs. The exact expectations and titles of these roles can vary from studio to studio. Leads, supervisors, associate directors, managers and producers. It is important to not assume any of those are the same across different studios or organizations.

The general rule of thumb is that a person can successfully manage five to nine people while still balancing some amount of discipline or project responsibilities. More than that, you are likely going to want to either share management responsibilities with other people or have a dedicated manager whose sole responsibility is that work. If you have someone in a full-time people management role, then 15–20 people is likely their limit.

With those numbers in mind, and depending on how the team is structured, you should be able to quickly define where you will need to add in leadership support roles. What can take some time and effort is finding and choosing the best person for each of these roles. Doing all of this well is a skillset separate from the expertise of a discipline, but it is no less important. You want someone who will treat management responsibilities as core to the success of the team and not as secondary responsibilities to their craft work. Remember the quote from Donnella Meadows at the beginning of this chapter. People in these roles, like your own, are in service to the team. Not the other way around. Some of the best people for these roles are the ones who are hesitant to take on the role because they understand the accountability and responsibility that go along with it. They realize the role isn't about their ego or growing their brand, but about supporting and advocating for their team. They are also more willing to

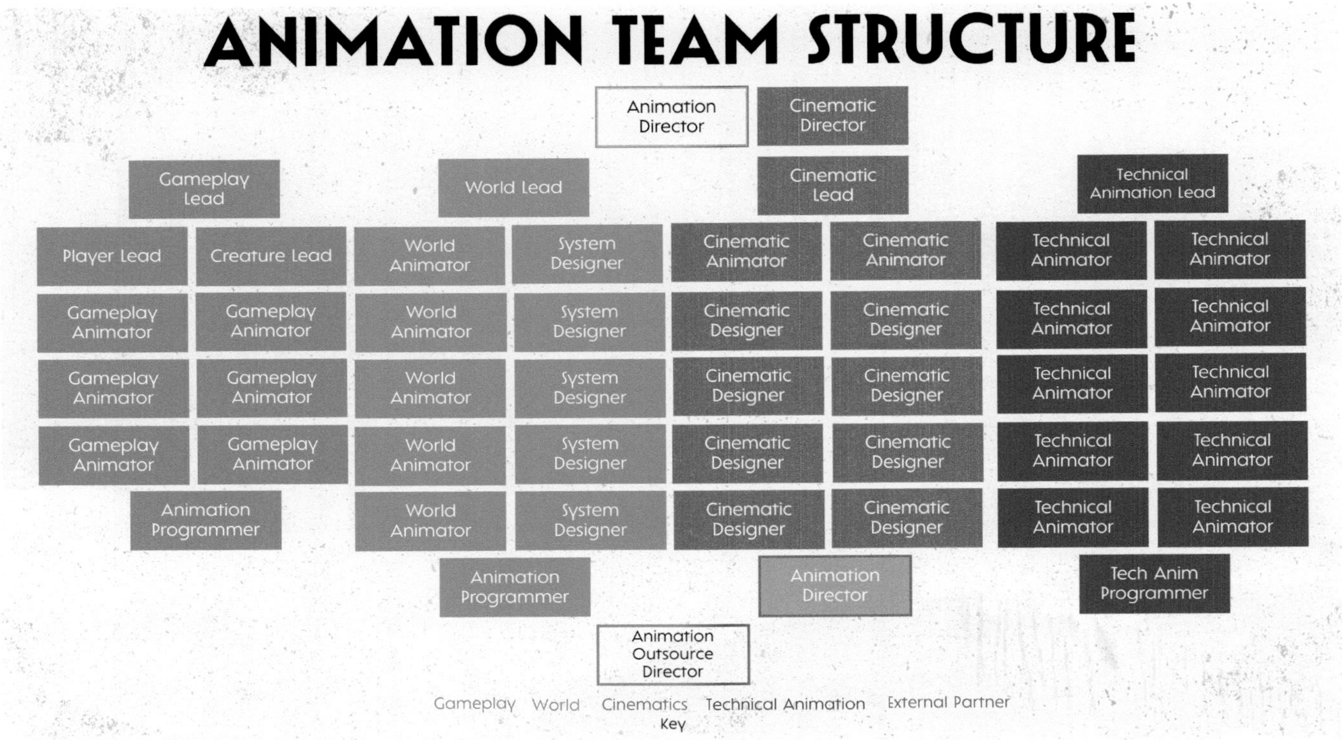

FIGURE 5.6   An example of an area-focused team structure used at BioWare on the *Dragon Age* team.

say, *'I don't know, but I know who to talk to, to find an answer'*, which is one of the most powerful tools a leader can wield. But that only comes from a place of trust and respect between a leader and a team.

You may also find some people more suited to mentoring the craft of a discipline than the more production-orientated aspects of leadership roles. And vice versa. Having clarity in roles and titles to allow for that is incredibly valuable, so that people can grow into leaders that best fit their natural strengths. Having a craft-focused supervisor role devoted to craft mentorship more than management can be incredibly valuable when you need to add subdiscipline or area groups within an existing group. For example, in gameplay animation teams, having a player supervisor and a creature or AI supervisor can help make sure both receive the unique, required attention often demanded of each at a craft level. And they can entirely focus on craft mentorship by keeping the people management responsibilities of those groups on the gameplay animation lead.

As a leadership team grows and evolves, it is important to remember that, like any other part of the team, how you structure a team defines how they will naturally communicate. So make sure that the natural tendencies of communication within the teams are accounted for in the leadership group. The communication amongst the leadership team can help cover gaps that will naturally form within the larger team.

EXTERNAL PARTNERS

Everything covered so far is doubly true when it comes to working with external partners, also known as outsource partners. Clear, consistent communication and structure are the defining features that can make or break the success of these endeavors. If there is an intention to work with external partners at any point in your project, you want to plan for that early in your team's structure and roles. Because, much like people management, there is a limit to how many external partners you can manage before you need to share those responsibilities or make it someone's full-time responsibility.

If it is one or two additional people, then it may be something you or another member of your team can take on as the primary point of contact, on top of other responsibilities. But when it grows beyond that, you want to establish clear structure and workflows; otherwise, both your internal and external team members will become frustrated, and the likelihood of a successful partnership will evaporate.

When it comes to thinking about external partners on your team, it is good to approach them on a spectrum. The lower cost studios often require more internal time to get up to speed and maintain consistency. The higher cost studios often require less internal time to get up to speed and maintain consistency. And then there are mid-tier studios between those two ends.

The other variable is the specific experience and expertise of the external team members you will be working with. Often times, external partners are thought of as someone you can bring in towards the end of a project to quickly ramp up support to meet deadlines. But just like when you hire someone internally, there is a ramp-up time required for the new team member to get up to speed on the intent of the project, the style and quality of the work, and the tools and workflows required to create and implement the work. All of this becomes more complicated with external partners, as they are less likely to have all of the internal resources available to them. Which is all to say, responsive and consistent communication with external partners is the number one priority for anyone assigned as their point of contact. This can either happen by embedding them as fully into your internal team as possible, similar to a contractor role. Or by having internal members take on the responsibility of communication and support from external team members.

When I moved into the director role on the *Dragon Age* team, the first position I pushed to open was for an Animation Outsource Manager, even though we were in early pre-production. You see, while I was only on *Anthem* for a short time, one of my primary responsibilities was supporting some external partners to help with the player exo-suits. Creatures and cinematics were already partnering with external teams, and there was more player animation work than the internal team could complete on their own. Knowing the tight deadlines and the added complexity of player animation needs, we brought in one of the more expensive studios to partner with because we needed people that had the highest likelihood of hitting the ground running. We didn't have clear documentation on workflows, easy integration of external partners to use our tools, clear file-transferring methods or consistent communication standards. Which meant we needed team members in approximate time zones to ours, studios with internal supervisors that have experience hitting a high-quality bar quickly, and English as a first language.

Even then, most of my day-to-day work involved integrating, testing and reviewing the work of two to three external partners. And when looking at creatures and cinematics, it was clear the people supporting the external partners in those areas were also dedicating a large portion of their day to that work. This meant key members of the internal team spent more time with our external partners than our internal team members. And if someone needed to take over supporting external partners because there was no consistency in how each person was managing the external team members, communication and quality would suffer.

So, when talking to team members about their expectations of me as animation director, a consistent point brought up was having a director that was focused on supporting the internal team's growth and needs. And the people who had been supporting external partners did not want to continue balancing that work with their other responsibilities. Creating a role on the team for a dedicated animation outsource manager was clearly the answer to solving this. The need for the role was clear, which led to the next phase of opening new roles.

PROJECT AND STUDIO BUY IN

At this point, you should know the team size you are likely to need, the leadership roles required to support that team, and how you will support external partners. And you have the research from investigating project needs, tech needs, competitive analysis and team expectations to back up your plan. It may be that what the studio and team have established in the past already supports what you need. But in some cases, what you may be proposing is a departure from past team structures, role responsibilities and studio expectations. In those cases, you will need more than numbers. You will need to show a plan for how you intend to get there from where the team is currently. And the *Dragon Age* animation team, between the creation of a world animation team and a dedicated outsource manager, is a great example of this.

The Animation Outsource Manager role was actually the easiest to get buy-in on, even early in pre-production. First, BioWare already had a dedicated team focused on external partner support, specifically in the form of 2d and 3d art. The studio had an understanding that if you wanted to scale up external support, you needed dedicated internal roles to be the points of contact and a consistent process for working with external teams. This was a clear example of the benefits of having a discipline-focused team. It also meant they understood that hiring someone to take on that role wasn't always easy to find. This all clearly aligned with the needs and issues that the team identified when it came to properly supporting animation outsourcing at any scale.

But why bring in this role so early in development, even if finding someone for the role isn't easy? That can be true of many disciplines and roles on a development team, but that doesn't guarantee or dictate success in opening a role during pre-production. It made sense here for two reasons. The first being that, in order to create consistent processes for working with external teams, those needed to be created early. We needed a list of all potential external partners, with their rates and specific skillsets. We needed consistent communication standards, defining what access they should have to platforms like email and slack but also documentation around workflows and tools. All of those take time to establish, especially if the person establishing them is new to the team and needs to first learn all of them for themselves.

The second is long-term cost savings. The sooner you have someone dedicated to this role, the sooner they can begin engaging with teams across the world that may not have the specific experience you need but, given the time and support, can be mentored to meet the quality and consistency expectations. This leads to long-term partnerships and more engaged experiences for everyone involved. So that if and when you need some last-minute support, you have additional options beyond the more expensive, expert studios that may not always have the availability or capacity required to provide support. A single internal team member, focused on this work, can likely support up to 20–25 external team members if given the time to build a foundation and grow the external team at a natural pace. When you present it that way to studio leadership, they will immediately see the long-term cost savings of having an extra internal salary at any stage of a project.

Getting buy-in for a new department, like world animation, was less straightforward. In that case, the ask is to expand the responsibilities and focus of the animation team. When viewed from the perspective of project leadership, the concern can be that this is going to require an expanded team size beyond what might have been originally projected in the budget. And by pulling experienced members of gameplay and cinematics, those areas may suffer to support the creation of something that was not required on past projects. This is where the investigation into project needs, tech needs and team expectations became valuable in buying the time needed to prove this out.

When talking to the tech experts on the team, the area highlighted as having the best workflow was cinematics. This meant support for cinematics during pre-production wasn't a priority, and members of that team interested in proving out custom scripted events were available. Another area often cited as a high point in Anthem was gameplay animation. And while there were additional tech needs there, unique to Dragon Age, having one or two members of gameplay that were specifically interested in proving out ambient NPC life and player interactions was something the gameplay team could afford during pre-production. On top of this, coming from a hard project that was not met with critical success, the team could use a morale boost. Allowing team members to work in new areas that interest them would be an opportunity to boost morale in the short term. Which ultimately meant project leadership could see the benefit of a short-term investment in this area during pre-production. With the understanding that team members were free to prove out the need for world animation until the needs of gameplay and cinematics required more support.

Again, having done the investigations into what those needs would be and approximately when those would come online, it meant there was a well-understood timeframe to prove out the value of creating this new department. The goal of this group was to prove that value before the time gameplay and cinematics needed to staff up, so that staffing would come from hiring new team members instead of dismantling the world animation team. We understood the long-term need was there, and if given a chance, the project and studio would see the need.

When presenting the team structure to studio leadership, showing the intended plan through different phases of pre-production, backed up by investigation findings and the above cases, gave clarity to the proposed plan (Figures 5.7–5.9).

Both investments ultimately paid off, as the team was able to create the workflows and cross-discipline partnerships that the studio previously lacked, both internally and externally, leveraging the structure that comes from both discipline and area focuses. Which is all to say, spending time understanding the needs of the project and team will help you understand and adapt to the opportunities afforded to you.

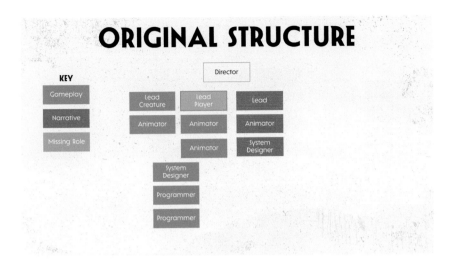

FIGURE 5.7   The initial *Dragon Age* animation team structure when I first came onto the project.

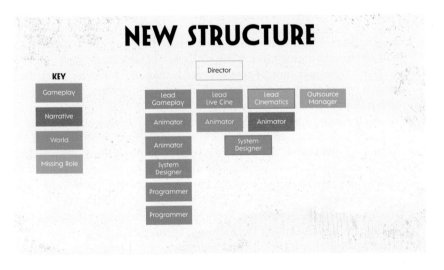

FIGURE 5.8   The restructured *Dragon Age* animation team during early pre-production, including the creation of a world animation team and the outsource manager role.

Now that you have a clear understanding of the project, the tech and the team, it is time to get into the area most animation directors are most eager to jump into: the style, tone and quality of the animation!

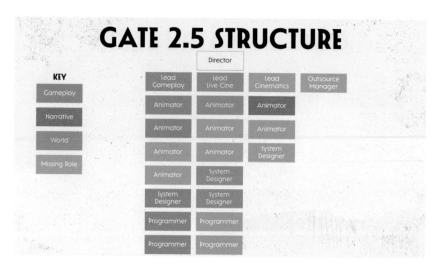

FIGURE 5.9 A chart showing how the *Dragon Age* animation team would likely need to grow over pre-production to support the intended features of the game.

NOTES

1 My go-to resource when talking to someone thinking about becoming a lead for the first time is Mike Acton's 2014 *Lead Quick Start Guide* blog post on GameDeveloper.com. If someone reads that and it doesn't scare them away, it means they are in the correct headspace to try taking on some leadership responsibilities.

2 While the cited quote from Donella Meadows' *Thinking in Systems: A Primer* (2008) is focused on leadership responsibilities within a system, the entire book has shaped the way I look at leadership and the creative process as a whole. The way she breaks down how everything in the world, both natural and manufactured, exists as a system makes this a must-read for all game developers.

3 You can find the Animation Team Size Calculator in a blog post on AnimState. It is something I update semi-regularly.

4 The Post-Project Animation Team Survey can also be found as a blog post on AnimState. It is on my list of things to integrate with the calculator more seamlessly. And maybe by the time you are reading this, it already has. Fingers crossed!

CHAPTER 6

Defining the Performance

W HEN PEOPLE THINK ABOUT animation direction, it is often the traditional craft of animation that is at the top of their minds. This makes sense, as that is ultimately what most people see and experience when they play the game. Which can make it hard to resist the desire to immediately jump to this part of the process. Likely, you already have some ideas or personal preferences on all of this, which is going to naturally influence the final vision as you spend months and years reviewing animation through the lens of your own personal tastes. But if you try to force aesthetic choices too soon without doing the investigative work before hand, you run the risk of creating a beautiful-looking cake that is hollow inside. Eventually, it will collapse on itself.

Which is why everything we have focused on up to this point has been about understanding what is required to create the entire cake, not only the frosting and decorations. So that when the time comes for people to encounter the cake, they can marvel at the beautiful creation before them and be greeted with something tasty and delightful when they cut into it. And maybe even be a bit surprised at how it subverts their expectations, but in a way that makes for a more complex and engaging experience overall.

So let's look at some specific ways to think about and engage with the possibility space around defining a project's animation vision. These should be treated as a sort of compass to use as you run down the branching alleyways

DOI: 10.1201/9781003356196-6

towards finding where the creative intent lives. As well as a map that you can use to give directions to others that need to arrive at the location where the intent lives. These are a combination of approaches predominately inspired by acting and dance practices, though adapted towards the needs of game animation. I would highly recommend further investigating any of the books or methods recommended here or in other chapters, as there is a wealth of thoughts, experiences and applications beyond what I touch upon. Humans have been focused on movement and emotion as a form of communication, study and creativity from some of our earliest moments.[1] There is a wealth of knowledge from different fields we have only begun to scratch the surface of including in our repertoire of references for interactive animation.

While there are several ways to approach finding the truth of a character and their performance, the goal of any approach ultimately aims to define and convey either the emotional or physical experiences of a character. While that is a rather reductive statement of the entire fields of philosophy, psychology and acting, for the intent of defining a high-level animation vision, emotion and physicality are the two vectors I like to use as starting points. While it is well worth the time to learn about the history of symbolic versus naturalistic acting,[2] I have found it valuable to think of defining a character's performance in two ways.

The first is having the emotional experience drive the action. This would be focusing on a character's personality, thoughts and emotional response to a moment. The second is committing to a physical action to drive the performance. This would be focusing on specific styles of dance, martial arts or other highly trained physical actions as the response to a moment. I like to think about this in terms of ballet. When a ballet dancer walks onto the stage, they convey a performance that comes from dedicated training of their body and mind to physically move in a very specific manner. Their goal and objective in the moment are in service of their training and the exact choreography of the scene. They are committing to the physical action of the performance. But when the ballet dancer walks off of the stage, they are no longer being driven by the physical action of the performance. Their goals and objectives are based on their own personal desires and experiences. Maybe they nailed their performance and they are excited to celebrate their success! Maybe they are distracted thinking about an awkward moment with another dancer, and they are nervous about seeing them after the performance. Off the stage, their actions are now driven by their emotional experiences.

Depending on the character, how they exist within the project, and the performers you are collaborating with, it will very much determine which of these approaches is best when defining and driving the animation vision.

EMOTIONALLY DRIVEN ACTIONS

When approaching a vision from the mindset of having the emotion drive the action, it makes sense to approach the needs of a character in a very actor-centric manner. And for this, I turn to the structure of acting, as conveyed by Ed Hooks in *Acting for Animators*.

> 'Acting Is ACTION in Pursuit of an OBJECTIVE, Trying to Overcome an OBSTACLE'

It can be easy, as an animation director, to focus on the *action* part of that definition. But that is the output of what we want the animators and capture performers to deliver on. In fact, focusing too much on the action in this instance will cause people to feel overdirected and micro-managed. The actual role of the animation director in this is to make sure there is always a clear *objective* and *obstacle* to inform the action. Which can be boiled down to the design or narrative *function* as discussed in Chapter 2. With the action being the *form* that conveys said function. How all the different bits of form come together to create a consistent performance is the goal of the animation vision. That vision can then be used as a way-point for everyone to start from and return to as the characters grow and become fully realized throughout the creation of the project across multiple disciplines and collaborators.

Character One Sheets

On *Agents of Mayhem*, we were presented with the challenge of having a large number of playable characters, each with their own unique personalities and abilities. Inspiration for characters could come from anyone on the team, so depending on the character, some had a deep backstory, some had only an amusing name and others had an appealing piece of concept art. To create a consistent performance for the character, we needed a way to see the art, the gameplay design, the high-level narrative goals, the character's personality and motivation all in one easy-to-digest source. With a Character One Sheet, we could quickly define all of the core, upstream aspects of a character and weave them together into a consistent performance. And while it may at first glance look like a lot, because of the consistency of the design and information, once you know what you are looking at, finding the necessary information becomes easy. This means that anytime an animator or actor became involved with a new character, this was an invaluable reference point for understanding the core of the character so that they could quickly orient themselves in the direction they could go with the performance. Let's start with Fortune (Figure 6.1).

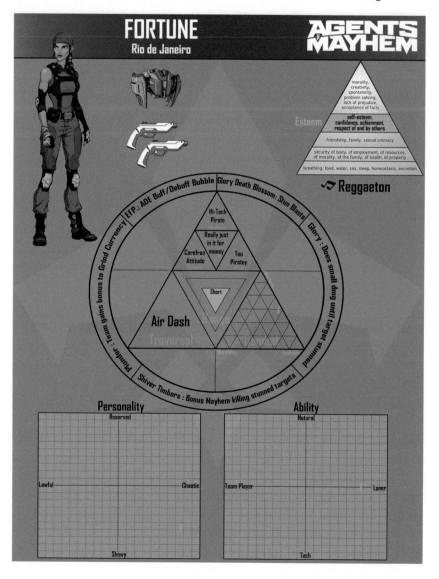

FIGURE 6.1 The full character one sheet created for the character Fortune.

As you can see, there is a fair bit here, so let's break down each section and the key pieces of information being conveyed.

First up, and pretty straight forward, is the character's name, where they are from, their concept art and their signature weapons and equipment. Fortune is from Rio de Janeiro and has her drone, Glory and two pistols (Figure 6.2).

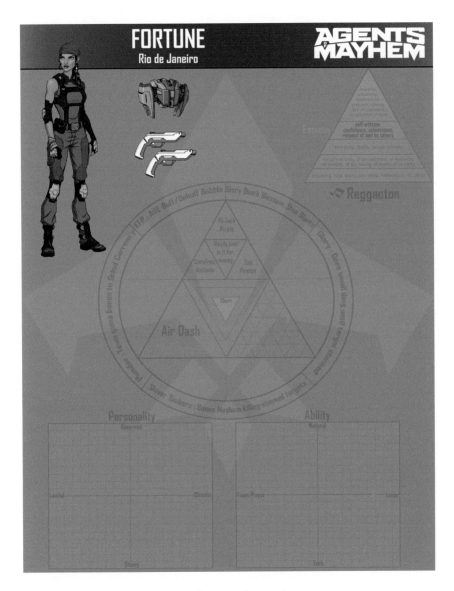

FIGURE 6.2   The top left corner of Fortune's one sheet.

Next is Maslow's Hierarchy of Needs. This was used to quickly define the driving objective of the character and define the core motivation as to why they are fighting the enemy forces of LEGION. The color of the level is then used in the rest of the sheet to make sure that the core objective is carried throughout everything. Fortune is all about esteem, driven by her confidence and achievement. She doesn't worry about or feel the need to fight for things like family, security or basic physiological needs (Figure 6.3).

Below Maslow's Hierarchy Triangle is the Agent's favorite music. Fortune's music of choice is Reggaeton. Figuring out their favorite music became one of my favorite elements of the process. A big part of a performance is being able to maintain the emotional state of the character. For actors, maintaining that emotional state throughout a shot or action can be measured in minutes or hours. For animators, it is hours, days or weeks. This is where knowing a character's favorite music becomes important. Listening to their favorite genre or artists while animating at a desk or capturing on a capture stage allows people to stay in a character's headspace for longer amounts of time. It can speak to and influence timing and personality choices. And unlock additional depth to their character as people search out new artists and become more immersed in the culture of the music. Even if it is a genre of music you dislike, as I initially did with Reggaeton, sticking with it can become an important part of the animation ritual when working on a character. For Fortune, if I was not listening to Reggaeton when animating or directing on the stage, it just didn't feel right (Figure 6.4).

Next is the design in the middle, which is the character's gameplay pillars. This combined chart is meant to show how the core agent's gameplay relates to the Agent's personality. Let's start with the ring around the outside of it (Figure 6.5).

This is the Ability Ring, broken into five sections. On the top left is the agent's *Special Ability*. This is meant to be used multiple times throughout a battle. Here, Fortune fires off an AOE blast. And in the top right section of the ring is the agent's *Mayhem Ability*. This is meant to be used once every few battles. Fortune has her drone create a death blossom-style AOE stun blast.

The bottom three sections of the ring are the Agent's passive abilities. While these often didn't require animations, it does speak to their playstyle and personality, which is important for animators to keep in mind as those help to define the character's in game performance and playstyle (Figure 6.6).

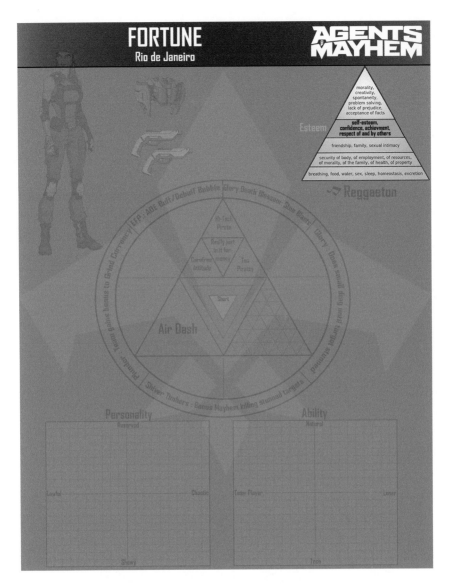

FIGURE 6.3 The top right corner of Fortune's one sheet.

Now looking at the triangle in the middle of the page, at the top is the *Traitforce*, which itself is broken into four sections. The triangle at the top is the character's must-have defined characteristic. This is their high-level pitch. Fortune is a Hi-Tech Pirate. The triangle at the bottom left is a strength of the character, in personality or gameplay, that we want

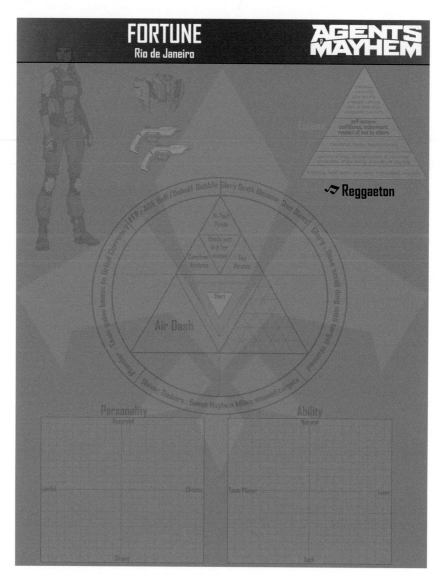

FIGURE 6.4   The musical preference shown of Fortune's one sheet.

to make sure is often highlighted. Fortune has a carefree attitude that we wanted to highlight whenever possible. The triangle at the bottom right shows potential pitfalls we can see the character falling into. These are areas we wanted to make sure we were always weary of, as it could make the character less enjoyable. We didn't want Fortune to come across as too much of a traditional pirate. No 'arrrrrrs' and 'ahoy mateys!' And finally,

FIGURE 6.5 The middle of Fortune's one sheet.

the triangle in the middle is the character's secret. This is something we don't overtly state to the player or in the game, or that the character would ever tell another soul, but something we use to help round out the character and give them depth when we are thinking about them. With Fortune, she is really just doing all of this for the money and tech (Figure 6.7).

FIGURE 6.6   The outer ring of element in the middle of Fortune's one sheet.

This triangle is the Agent's unique traversal type. For Fortune, this means she can air-dash (Figure 6.8).

The Range Triangles in the middle indicate at what range the agent is best suited with their weapons and abilities. Fortune is a short-range character (Figure 6.9).

FIGURE 6.7 The top part of the triangle in the middle element of Fortune's one sheet.

The Combat Triangle defines what play style and role the Agent's abilities and weapons fall within with regards to Mayhem, Lethality and Durability. Fortune is between Mayhem, which is how much they should use and rely on their abilities, and Lethality, how much damage they can output (Figure 6.10).

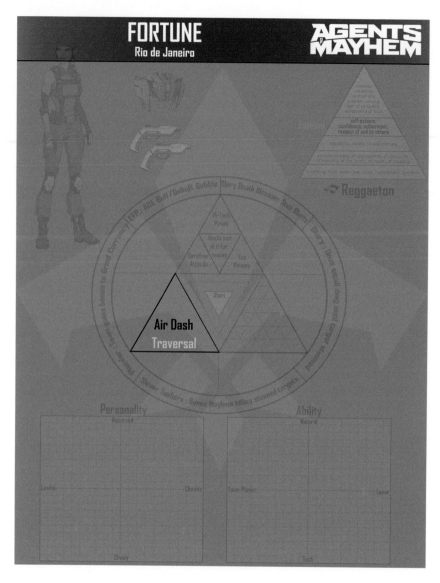

FIGURE 6.8   The left part of the triangle in the middle element of Fortune's one sheet.

And finally, we have our coordinate graphs, the inherent personality and ability of the characters. On each line of the graph, there are two opposing sets of traits. You then plot the character on the graph in terms of where they best fit (Figure 6.11).

FIGURE 6.9 The middle part of the triangle in the middle element of Fortune's one sheet.

On the left is the Personality Graph, which, from top to bottom, has *Reserved vs Showy*. This describes how flamboyant an Agent is. Are they more willing to be the strong, silent type or are they super boisterous in everything they do? Fortune is pretty damn showy.

FIGURE 6.10 The right part of the triangle in the middle element of Fortune's one sheet.

From left to right *Lawful vs Chaotic*. This describes how much an Agent follows a sense of order. Are they more honorable or are they more reckless? Fortune is rather chaotic (Figure 6.12).

On the right is the Ability Graph, where from top to bottom we have *Natural vs Tech*. This describes the Agent's inherent ability set. Are they

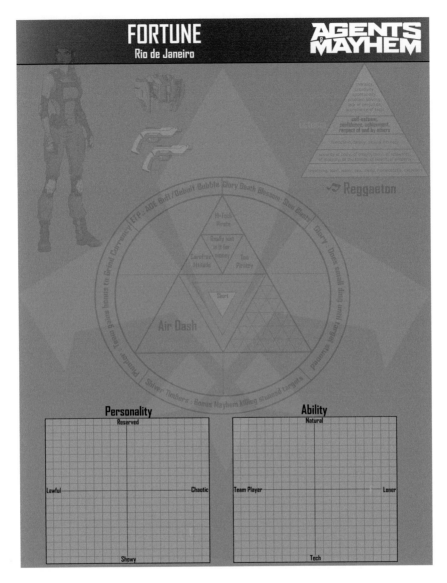

FIGURE 6.11   The bottom graph elements of Fortune's one sheet.

naturally capable or do they rely primarily on their tech? Fortune is right in the middle, meaning that she is as naturally capable and gifted as she is using tech.

Next, from left to right, is *Team Player vs Loner*. This describes how well an Agent gets along with others. Are they the type that rallies around teammates or do they prefer to hang out on their own? Fortune

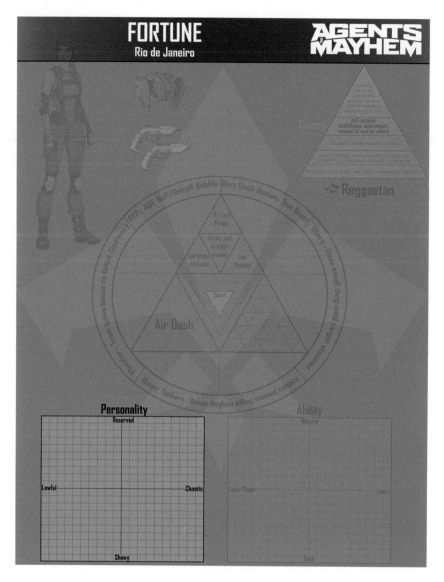

FIGURE 6.12   The bottom left graph of Fortune's one sheet.

is much more of a loner, reflecting both her placement in Maslow's Hierarchy and her secret (Figure 6.13).

So, stepping back, once you know what all of this means, you can get a really great read on who Fortune is, in terms of breadth and depth, very quickly. For reference, here is Rama's One Sheet. Read over it before reading the intent that is meant to be conveyed (Figure 6.14).

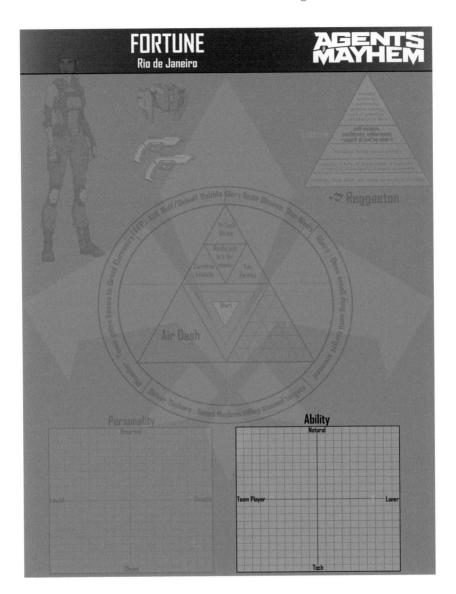

FIGURE 6.13   The bottom right graph of Fortune's one sheet.

After reading over this, you now know that Rama uses her bow to fight and secure her homeland of India. She uses different types of arrows and enjoys crunk music. She is a rather lawful and reserved character and, by her nature, a team player, using the tech available to her to help others. The more of these we made, the more each character came alive with a

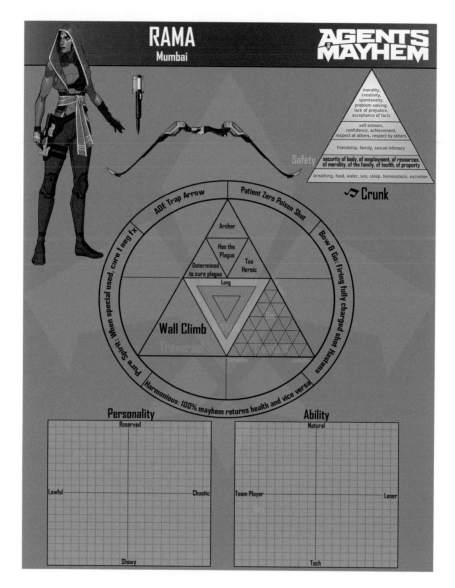

FIGURE 6.14   Rama's character one sheet.

consistent level of depth and unique personality. This especially became helpful when we would cast and prepare actors for capture.

When working with actors for mocap, finding every opportunity to sell the tone and experience of the game or character is key. Playing the character's favorite music on the stage was part of this. And beyond that, the one sheets were designed to recall the sort of character cards that would be included with action figures from the 80's. When we would hand over these sheets, along with any additional references we felt added value (e.g. 3d character models, additional concept art and a full biography), we would put them in a folder with the character's code name on it and confidential stamped on the front. All of this was meant to help the actor more quickly step into the headspace of the character and world.

With this style of a one sheet, you can quickly pack a lot of information into a single source of truth that people on the team can learn to read and understand quickly. The trick of course is that you will need to take the time to create a one sheet that works best for your project and characters. This can require a lot of iteration with design, art and narrative to realize. Which means you need to be creating enough characters with a consistent design or narrative function at their core that applying this as a template is possible and worth the effort. This makes one sheets fantastic when creating a breadth of characters available for players to engage with, such as fighting games, MOBAs or hero shooters.

Personality Trait Videos

When you find the need to further flesh out the personality and depth of a character's performance beyond what a one sheet can offer, a personality traits video can be a fantastic option. This is similar to the competitive analysis video in Chapter 4, but instead of gameplay features, you are using personality traits as your reference point. The intent of this is to take what is likely a lengthy biography and convey that in a 30- to 60-second montage video. That video can then be shared with any animator or actor that is involved in bringing the character's performance to life. The most important constraints to pay attention to when making these videos are to define the correct traits and keep the video under 1 minute.

The traits should be defined in collaboration with animation and narrative. Depending on how far along a character is and who is most responsible for the character's realization, this could be a combination of the head of narrative, the head of the project, the head of cinematics, the head of art, the individual writer, the animator and yourself. The more people involved in this process, the longer it can take, so if the group starts to become too large, it is important to identify the most key and vocal contributors to the character and rapidly iterate with them as much as possible to define the core needs and intent they are specifically attached to.

This is where having a constraint on the number of traits is valuable, as it forces people to prioritize what is most important to the core of the character. While there is obviously no limit to the number of traits you can include, I have found three traits to be the magic number, as they can drive early conversations on what the defining motivations and emotional responses are for a character. This is the narrative function required to realize the form of action the character will take in their performance.

As an example of this process in action, we will look at a personality trait video for Hazel from *South of Midnight*. While this is obviously a valuable process when first realizing a character, by the time I joined the project, Hazel had already existed for years. So this was as much an opportunity for me to better understand her as a character as it was to define the animation direction and realization moving forward into full production. Because of how much work had already gone into creating her, we started with four traits instead of three.

- *Impulsive*

- *Stubborn*

- *Clever*

- *Irreverent*

Once you have the traits, it is also worth asking if there are any characters, fictional or real, that have inspired the creation of this character. Often times, there is someone specific people are thinking about when they first began to write or draw, to find their voice or inspiration. This is super helpful to know, as it will give you some immediate reference points in starting the search for the next step, which is finding video clips and references to match and illustrate the traits. There is often already an existing fan base for almost any character from TV or movies, many with themed montages or favorite moments already compiled for you to get started with. This can be the immediate momentum you are looking for to get the trait video moving forward, but you do not want to stop there. Often, those characters that inspire do not match all the traits you need to define. Or there are additional core traits that define the referenced character that you do not want associated with your character. This is where curating your own personal list of characters, actors and reality personalities can become very valuable. The more people, shows and creations you can watch and absorb across all genres and formats, the more starting points you will be able to draw from when working on a new character.

But even if you have a large personal library of characters to draw inspiration from, it is important at this stage to spend time researching the traits and inspirations of the referenced characters. What are the synonyms for each trait? Search for characters, real or fictional, that match those synonyms. Watch and listen to interviews with the actors and creators of those referenced characters about where they drew their creative influence. With these trait videos, because they reference clips of other characters and people, it can be easy to fall into creating a copy of another character by creating a video that is too prescriptive or stereotypical if you too heavily rely on only one reference point. So cast a wide net on your first cut. If the reference clip feels appropriate to one of the traits, that is what ultimately matters.

In the case of Hazel, characters from *Ozark, Zombieland, Sex Education* and *Winter's Bone* were early reference points, especially in terms of Stubborn and Irreverent traits. That helped to establish an early direction in those instances, but also highlighted clear gaps when informing who Hazel was in total. Looking to find the limits of the character, I pulled in references from *Euphoria*, the *Saved by the Bell* reboot, *Friday Night Lights, Doctor Who, Step Up: High Water, and WandaVision*. All of these vary greatly in terms of tone and realization, but that is fine, as what you are looking for are moments of truth that match your character. It is the gestalt of these moments that ultimately defines the character.

From this point, you likely have many, many minutes worth of videos to dig through. Within your video editing software of choice, begin to edit the clips into groups that best match each trait. Sometimes everything just clicks, and the gestalt of the character readily appears before you. But just as likely, you may find some clips, when isolated from the context of the larger video, don't match the intended trait as well as you thought. Or you may be lacking clips of a specific trait. You may also find that a lot of the clips that feel right for the character don't match any of the traits. In either case, getting together a first rough cut is valuable to check back in with the key stakeholders of the character. Which is where having a template for these videos is valuable. Though nothing as robust as the One Sheet template is required here (Figure 6.15).

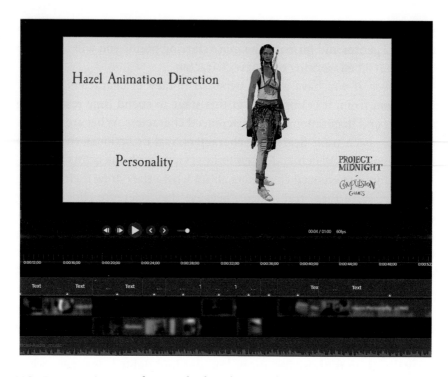

FIGURE 6.15   A screenshot inside the editing software showing the number of clips and how they are formatted for Hazel in *South of Midnight*.

For these video templates, having a title screen with the character's name, concept art and a callout that this is their personality trait video is what you are looking for. From there, labeling each clip with the overlay text of the trait is the other necessary element. And for clips that feel true to the character but not the trait, you can either create a new trait that they align with or label those as miscellaneous. That should be enough to share and foster conversations around the next steps. It could be that you are well on track and given a thumbs up to do a final pass with only minor notes to address. It could be after looking at the video, you all realize the traits and/or references within are not correct. That is perfectly normal, as it highlights miscommunications and misunderstandings at the core of the character in a time and format where it is easy to discuss and adjust. This will also give you key insight into the collaborative process you are likely to expect with team members as you continue together to develop this character and others. So do not be afraid to change keywords, reference characters or clips at any point, as all of this is informing not just who the character is but also who they are not. Which is just as valuable as defining who they are.

Hazel's personality video went through four different iterations, each featuring significantly different characters and clips than the last. The clips that made it from the first to the last are few, with each addition and removal informing valuable conversations around the overall tone and perception of the character that the video conveyed. And it also highlighted and clarified any unconscious biases that presented themselves within the referenced characters or clips.

This all helps as you work on each draft, continually refining the edit to cut out unnecessary clips. These could be clips that slow down the overall pacing, repeat something another clip better conveys, or are too prescriptive of another character or actor's approach that may influence the future performance too much. Remember that the end goal here is to create a 30- to 60-second video, which can be a surprisingly few number of clips. The time constraint of the video is as important as the number of traits and the variety of reference points.

It was a mixture of these constraints that led to significant changes after the third iteration of Hazel's video. It was clear that the tone and core of the character had been stretched too far across the four different traits. There were elements that resonated, but others were still missing when talking to people about who Hazel was. And getting a cut of the video to be less than 90 seconds was proving to be a challenge. This led to proposing three new traits that better embodied Hazel's core personality.

- *Determined*

- *Spontaneous*

- *Genuine*

Through using *Determined* and *Spontaneous* as synonyms for *Stubborn* and *Impulsive*, it allowed aspects of *Clever* and *Irreverent* to fit within those new traits. Which made room for *Genuine* to be added, which gave additional depth and earnestness to Hazel. And it allowed for an edit that was exactly 60 seconds long.[3]

Another important element in these videos is the musical choice you make. The audio can set the tone from the outset, giving you something to time the title card elements to, as well as being the glue that holds various moments and characters together. It can also work to add depth to imply any secondary traits you want people to emotionally feel, but not an outright signal. With Hazel's video, the first two iterations featured song choices that were informed by either montage videos of reference characters or the project as a whole. But the perfect song came when people on the team who were closer to her age and background proposed music suggestions they thought Hazel would listen to. Which, while different from the tone of the project, helped to better set Hazel apart on her own.

Remember that the entire point of this video, like the character one sheet, is to provide a point of reference for people to immediately align and orient towards. It is common for multiple people and actors to be involved in delivering a character's performance. And each person brings their own personal experiences and creative choices to that realization. What makes a character stand out is when everyone involved in its performance can instill genuine, emotional truth. These methods exist to give someone new to the character a clear direction on where to start when looking for that truth. And a guidepost to return to for someone who has traveled too far off course in search of it.

PHYSICALLY DRIVEN ACTIONS

When it comes to personality and emotion, there tends to be more of a shared vocabulary between all of the creative disciplines. But when it comes to directing physicality, the vocabulary fractures. Animators will often perform a physical action to convey their intent. Designers may reference actions from other games. And the descriptive words that are used, such as heavy, smooth or cool, are too broad or too often loaded with unnecessary context to be helpful. There is however an entire way of describing motion that has been used by dancers, actors and athletes for decades, known as Laban Movement Analysis (LMA) (Figure 6.16).

LMA is an entire practice of study that looks to describe the physical motion of the body and the intent behind it. It is multi-faceted and well worth exploring[4] beyond what I write here. I am going to focus on only one aspect of it, which is the Effort or Dynamic Elements. And more specifically, how it can be adapted to define and inform the physical actions of a performance in an intentional way. Which is all to say, this is influenced by LMA, but not actually LMA.

Effort Elements take two opposing terms, such as light and strong, and assign one of the terms to an action. Other elements include sustained and sudden. Or free and bound. The value of this approach comes when you

ACTION	TIME	WEIGHT	SPACE
Punch	sudden	strong	direct
Dab	sudden	light	direct
Slash	sudden	strong	indirect
Flick	sudden	light	indirect
Press	sustained	strong	direct
Glide	sustained	light	direct
Wring	sustained	strong	indirect
Float	sustained	light	indirect

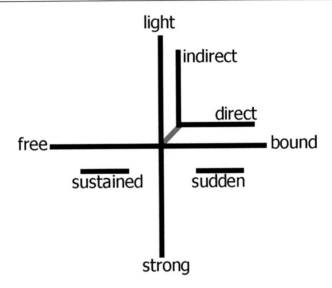

FIGURE 6.16   Example of Laban Movement Analysis effort actions and graph.

apply multiple opposing terms to an action or performance. Think of how a sustained, strong action would be realized as opposed to a sudden, strong action. When working on characters in which the commitment to the physical action is driving the performance of a character, being able to communicate in these terms gives clarity to the intent without being too physically prescriptive, as if you were to act or describe a specific motion. This is how you can provide direction for physicality with an eye towards the function, allowing the animator or actor to supply the form of their choosing.

While LMA has specific terms that they stick to for their Elements, in an effort to open up the possibility space a bit more, I like to use the term Movement Elements to offer more flexibility to the vision. To fully explain why I will present the process of defining the animation vision for player factions, as originally conceptualized as a way to give a distinct visual identity to the *Dragon Age* franchise.

It started, as many action games do, by looking for references for how the player can move and attack in a way that can make them stand out and feel unique. The high-level animation vision for the game was to *Boldy Reflect Choice and Intent*. And one of the most long-lasting choices the player would make in the game was the choice of their faction. Having previously worked on *Lord of the Rings* and *Elder Scrolls* games, it was clear we would need to move beyond the traditional Historical European Martial Arts (HEMA) that is most often associated with high fantasy if we wanted to boldly reflect the choice and intent behind each faction. We needed to open up the possibility space for the team to be able to reference as many unique fight styles as possible while clearly defining a unique vision for each faction that made it immediately stand out. However, I was not the most knowledgeable about martial arts in general, so I started my journey by watching videos for every fight style listed on Wikipedia.[5] Watching videos of different fight styles from all over the world was exciting, but it also quickly became overwhelming. I needed a way to evaluate, organize and classify each fight style in a way that made sense. This is when I turned to Movement Elements.

I created a list of each fight style, with links to videos that best represented what made them unique. From there, I assigned some common movement elements I saw across them. Were they often in a high or low stance? Was the motion often broad or contained? Fluid or staccato? Were they always active between each action or would they remain still? I wasn't worried about locking down any specific terms yet, as new styles might highlight a new element upon further observation.

Once I had gone through every fight style, I returned to the narrative, design and art intent established for each faction. There had already been a core team of designers, artists and writers in early pre-production before animation joined the project. This meant they had already defined the intent between each of the different factions, which they were using as a foundation to drive the creative choices they were each making for their respective disciplines.

I assembled the visions together in the following format:

- *Faction Name*
  - *Design/Class Intent*
    - *Art and Narrative Elements*

I then went through and bolded the specific elements that felt most associated with how they would move.

- *Grey Wardens*
  - *Warrior: Juggernaut, Tank, Fighter, Knight*
    - *Heroic: Shiny, **Noble**, **Professional***
    - *Tainted: **Stained**, Infected, **Enhanced***
    - *Slayer: Utility, Worn, **Disciplined***

- *Antivan Crows*
  - *Rogue: Assassin, Thief, Ninja*
    - *Killer: **Control**, Polished, Dark, Sharp*
    - *Seductive: **Elegant**, Romantic, Sumptuous*
    - *Theatrical: **Dramatic**, Expensive, **Flourish***

- *Veil Jumpers*
  - *Mage/Rogue: Druid, Hunter, Shaman, Ranger*
    - *Protector: **Traditional**, Anachronistic, Preserver*
    - *Hunter: **Hidden**, Survivalist, **Predatory***
    - *Mystic: **Natural**, Magic, Enchanted*

- *Shadow Dragons*
  - *Mage/Warrior: Melee Mage, Wizard, Healer*
    - *Secretive: **Shadowy**, Mysterious, Dark, **Deceptive**, **Shrouded***
    - *Underground: Utilitarian, **Improvised**, Resistance*
    - *Elemental Magic: **Fire and Ice**, Crystals, Arcane Knowledge*

- *Lords of Fortune*
  - *Rogue/Warrior: Pirate, Barbarian, Berserker*

- *Treasure: **Flashy, Eclectic**, Decadent, Colorful*
- *Fighter: **Taunting, Bold**, Relaxed, Brave*
- *Explorer: **Athletic**, Infiltrator, Collector*

- *Mourn Watch*

  - *Mage: Necromancer, Dark Mage, Lich*

    - *Death: **Corpses, Burial, Ceremonial**, Morbid*
    - *Science: Instruments, **Precision, Procedure, Measurement***
    - *Magic: **Ritual**, Spirit, Reanimation*

With these terms identified, I could then attach the movement elements of each faction to the core design, narrative and art elements. This is an important and necessary step in order to create a flexible animation vision in terms of form, because the function is entirely informed by the core. New abilities, different equipment and variable body sizes. None of those would require a change in the animation vision because the motion elements are not attached to that. The motion elements are attached to the core intent of the design, narrative and art. To significantly impact the animation vision at that point would mean a change to the core of one of the other visions, which would ripple throughout every other discipline. This meant it was as solid a foundation as could ever exist in a collaborative creation.

Looking back at the Movement Elements and comparing them against the bolded terms, the following list of five contrasting elements took shape.

- *High vs Low*
- *Broad vs Contained*
- *Fluid vs Staccato*
- *Active vs Still*
- *Effort vs Effortless*

Like with the LMA elements, one of each pair is to be exclusively assigned. But instead of doing so on a per action basis, they are assigned to the entirety of the faction's movement. To explain the thought process in action, let's look at the Grey Wardens.

The bolded terms for the Grey Wardens were Noble, Professional, Stained, Enhanced and Disciplined. These can then be directly used to inform the choice for each pair of Movement Elements. A high stance speaks to being Noble and Professional. Contained displays a sense of being Disciplined. Staccato betrays the Stained nature of how they became Enhanced. It still speaks to their Disciplined nature. And Effort matches well the Stained and Enhanced traits. This meant the Grey Warden's Movement Elements were:

- *High*

- *Contained*

- *Staccato*

- *Still*

- *Effort*

This can then be done for each faction. The ultimate goal is to have enough Movement Elements available that can be appropriately defined by core intent so that each faction has its own unique combination of Movement Elements. One way to quickly visualize this for people was by creating an area chart in Excel. By assigning each Faction a 1 or 0 to the appropriate motion element, highlighting all of the cells and inserting an area chart, I had an immediate visual representation of how the factions all complimented and contrasted one another (Figures 6.17 and 6.18).

	Grey Wardens	Shadow Dragons	Mourn Watch	Antivan Crows	Veil Jumpers	Lords of Fortune
High	1	0	1	1	0	0
Broad	0	1	0	1	0	1
Fluid	0	0	1	1	0	1
Active	0	1	0	1	0	1
Effort	1	0	0	0	1	1
Low	0	1	0	0	1	1
Contained	1	0	1	0	1	0
Staccato	1	1	0	0	1	0
Still	1	0	1	0	1	0
Effortless	0	1	1	1	0	0

FIGURE 6.17 A screenshot showing the simple Excel setup to create an area chart.

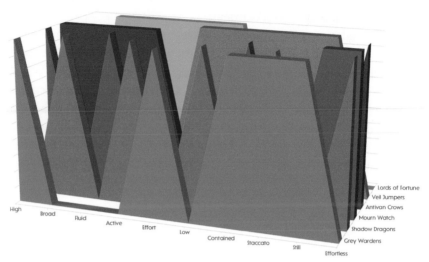

FIGURE 6.18 An area chart that shows how each faction plots uniquely across the separate movement elements.

Once each faction's Movement Elements were defined, it was time to go back to the fight styles and see which matched the Movement Elements assigned to each faction. And this is where things get fun! Because each faction had their own unique combination of Movement Elements, the fight styles that could be referenced were immediately diverse while naturally fitting the Movement Elements of the faction. And because we were focused on consistent Movement Elements more than any individual martial arts style or culture, we could mix and match with anything that aligned with the elements. The Grey Wardens, instead of being only influenced by traditional HEMA fight styles,[6] could also incorporate elements of Māori fight styles.[7] The Crows were able to draw influence from both Kalaripayattu,[8] a fight style from India, as well as XMA,[9] which mixes gymnastics with mixed martial arts. The Veil Jumpers were able to pull from various Shaolin animal styles[10] and Singlestick,[11] a French form of stick fighting. The Lords of Fortune were able to draw from South American,[12] Cambodian[13] and Turkish[14] fight styles.

But beyond martial arts, you can bring in any form of movement. Dance, music conductors, athletics. Everything is on the table as long as the form matches the function of the Movement Elements. This became core to defining the more magical factions, using modern dance styles[15] for the Shadow Dragons and orchestra conductors[16] for the Mourn Watch. But then elements of krunk[17] could also be added to the Grey Wardens, along with ballet[18] to the Antivan Crows. By adding the defined constraints of Movement Elements, as informed by the core fantasies of the factions as defined by design, narrative and art, the possibility space actually became MORE open for what was possible on the project. Suddenly, Hip-Hop Magicians and Ballet Assassins were the animation vision. Not as mere novelties based only on what looks cool, but intentional choices that actually speak to the core of the factions. Each faction became a cake that would look amazing and unique. And when cut into, the taste is a delightful surprise that both complements and subverts expectations.

Of note, regardless of whether you have emotional experience or physical experience driving the performance, when it comes time to cast actors and performers for capture, it is key to lean into both their training and natural sensibilities. For emotionally driven performances, cast actors that have dramatic experience so that they can quickly find the truth of each character required of them on the day of the shoot. If you do need to cast a stunt actor for emotionally driven experiences, cast someone whose natural personality matches the traits of the character they are playing. And when having physically driven experiences, cast someone who is well trained in the style of movement required. For instance, when someone has spent years learning ballet, their training can be felt even during their non-performative actions. The way they do something as mundane as flip a light switch is likely to employ their muscle memory, making it more naturally graceful than someone acting as if they know ballet. You may not always have the luxury of casting specialists for every shoot, every time, but when you do, make the most of the truth they will bring to the role. Also consider that, because you are branching out to specialists, this may very likely be their first time on a capture stage. This makes the need to be able to clearly direct the intent all the more important, as it may take them more time to get into the groove than other, more experienced capture performers you have worked with. But the investment is worth it, as the choices and experience they bring will instill a unique spark you are unlikely to have had otherwise.

Ultimately, the benefits of clearly defined traits and elements yield ongoing rewards. The breadth of talent you will be able to work with naturally expands. The opportunities for reference and research keep you naturally curious about new experiences and learnings. And while adding structure and constraints, at first glance, can make it feel like you are limiting the possibility space, what you are actually doing is focusing in on opportunities you didn't know about until pointed in the right direction. By narrowing a specific performance within a 45° cone, you are allowing the other 315° left to be explored by other characters. Ultimately, enabling the team and project to take part in having a purpose and opportunity to engage with the full 360° of human experiences.

NOTES

1 Augustín Fuentes's book *The Creative Spark: How Imagination Made Humans Exceptional* (2017) makes the case that it is humans' capacity for creativity that drove evolution. It also provides some insight and overlaps with the discussion from Chapter 3 around Effort and Value, as it traces the history of trade craft and mentorship back to the use of breaking and flaking stone tools for cutting. Some of our earliest methods of learning and creating were by watching, practicing, failing and growing.

2 Isaac Butler's *The Method: How the Twentieth Century Learned to Act* (2022) is focused on the history of Stanislavski's System and the ways others engaged with and adapted it. Which is reason enough to read this. But it is also a fantastic look at the history of creative, cultural and political factors that have influenced the craft of acting in ways we now take for granted.

3 You can find the reference Hazel video as part of the supplemental package on the book's website. It is titled Video_PersonalityTraits_Hazel. Like any reference material or documentation, this should be seen as a moment of time in the development process and not an expectation of 1:1 reality. Early vision direction, such as this, should be seen as someone pointing to a location in the distance, and depending on the path between where you are and where you are pointing, the path will almost certainly need to wind and adjust as you learn more along the way.

4 To learn more about LMA, you should check out Laban for Animators. Leslie Bishko is trained in LMA and has specifically developed a course as it pertains to animation. She can speak to the entire breadth and value of LMA beyond the crude adaptation I present here.

5 As you can see on the Wikipedia – List of Martial Arts, there are so many martial arts and most games have only scratched the surface. *The following reference notes are all the titles of videos demonstrating the different movement styles I listed in the Physically Driven Actions section of this chapter.*

6 Akademia Szermierzy-Fior di Battaglia: Chapter II (The Guards of the Sword) (YouTube).

7 Taiaha-Martial arts of the Maori (YouTube).

8 Kalarippayattu Sword and Shield Fight (YouTube).

9 XMA & Tricking Seminar with Master Ryan Phillips (YouTube).

10 5 animal styles kung fu (YouTube).

11 Single stick fight demonstration (YouTube).
12 KINESTECIA 2 EN EL NORTE DEL CAUCA: Escuela de grima con machete "los emprendedores" (YouTube).
13 Bokator: techniques et démonstration (YouTube).
14 Turkish Martial Arts – TÜRK DÖVÜŞ SANATI (YouTube).
15 "7 RINGS"-Ariana Grande|Janelle Ginestra Choreography (YouTube).
16 Arturo Márquez – Danzón No. 2 (Alondra de la Parra, L'Orchestre de Paris) (YouTube).
17 El Chapo-The Game – @Willdabeast – Choreography – #buckSeries (YouTube).
18 Kitri Variation Act 1: Zakharova, Osipova, Nunez (YouTube).

CHAPTER 7

Defining the Animation Style

O N TOP OF THE emotional and physical performances of a character, there is the animation style itself to be defined. Using the definition of art as *'communicating an idea with creative intent'*, the style would be the specific way in which the intent is being communicated. It is the language, inflection and pace you use to communicate your intent. In terms of animation, this translates to posing, motion and timing as the building blocks used to define a style.

How those building blocks can be used to convey a specific style can be incredibly subjective to define. For clarity of communication around style, I will be using a coordinate graph with *abstract to realism* on one axis and *constrained to boundless* on the other. Abstract to realism speaks to the level of detail and specificity in the representation of the style. Constrained to boundless refers to imposed limits or constraints around how the building blocks are used. Plotting the elements will allow for a visualization of the different styles to be discussed below, as well as the ability to specifically plot timing, posing and motion in relation to the overall style (Figure 7.1).

The examples in that chart are meant as a quick, high-level reference, but certainly not the limits of those axes. Each axis, like all art styles, is continually evolving and pushing the boundaries of what is possible. Furthermore, when you break down the elements of style, timing, posing

DOI: 10.1201/9781003356196-7

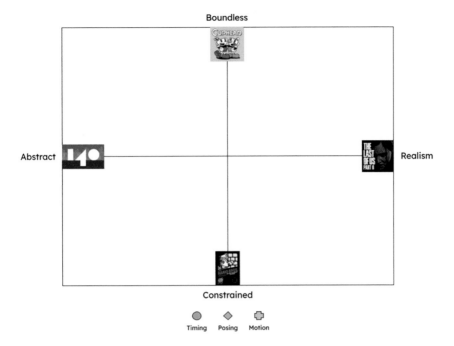

FIGURE 7.1 A coordinate graph used to categorize styles between abstract and realism, constrained and boundless, with different games at the end point of each axis for reference. At the bottom is the key to showing which shape represents timing, posing and motion when plotted on the chart.

and motion, you will see they do not perfectly sit in a single location, which can also make charting a game's full style as one point a bit contentious and confusing. Which is where plotting those individually becomes powerful. By breaking down each of those four titles, you can see a clearer representation of their true style (Figures 7.2–7.5).

We will discuss each of these in more detail within the high-level style groups they can be considered a part of. But I would hope that you already can see the value and opportunities that are made clear when approaching the topic of style and how best to define and communicate it. Both for this book and when discussing style on your project. For collaborative creations, style can be a tricky ingredient to discuss or lock down, as it can be wildly variable and dependent on a host of different factors across the project. The tools, the people, the project vision, the art direction and more can all influence and define the animation style beyond your own desires. This is where the graph can help align everyone at a high level.

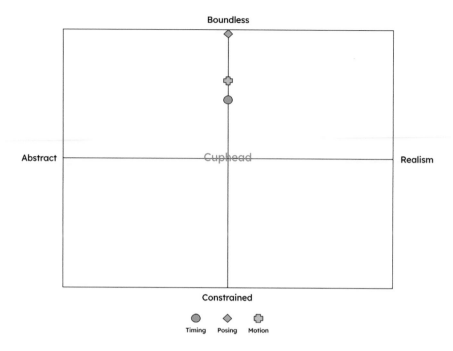

FIGURE 7.2　A coordinate graph used to plot the elements of style for *Cuphead*.

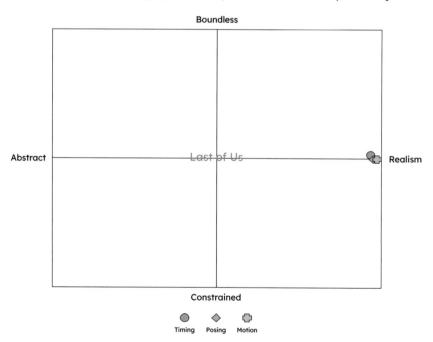

FIGURE 7.3　A coordinate graph used to plot the elements of style for *The Last of Us 2*.

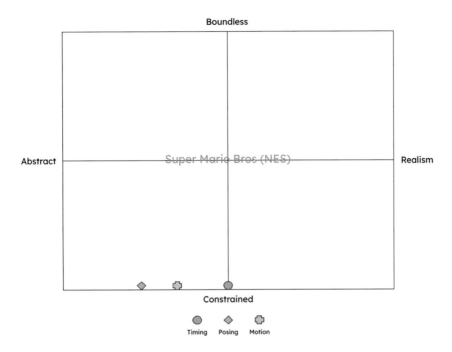

FIGURE 7.4 A coordinate graph used to plot the elements of style for *Super Mario Bros (NES)*.

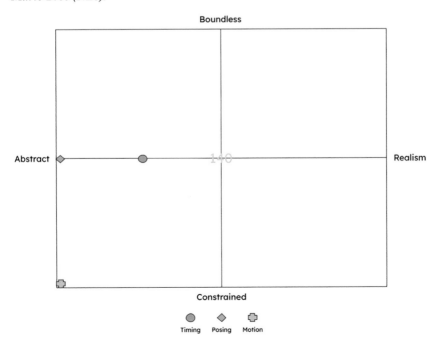

FIGURE 7.5 A coordinate graph used to plot the elements of style for *140*.

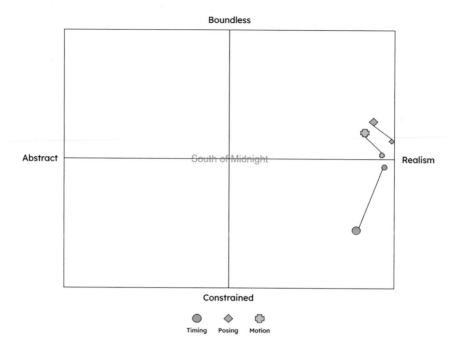

FIGURE 7.6 A coordinate graph used to plot the elements of style for *South of Midnight*.

It is also possible to expand each of these style elements across a spectrum. To do this, you can classify the larger shapes as extreme, with the smaller shapes for actions that are more grounded (Figure 7.6).

So in the case of animation on *South of Midnight*, the more grounded actions, such as walk and jog, would be classified by the smaller shapes, closer to full realism. The more expressive actions, such as the more extraordinary actions, would be at the extreme of the style, represented by the larger shapes. But there are other actions, such as jumping, that do not fit that binary, based on both the stylistic choices desired by the animator and the required functionality of the game. Which means those actions can exist anywhere on the line between the grounded and expressive points. Likewise, not all actions need to be at equal distance between the two points of each style element, just as each style element is not at equal distance from one another. This should allow for flexibility in meeting game needs as well as aesthetic and creative desires.

The other aspect to keep in mind in regards to style, before we dig into specifics, is how best to apply it. The following style groups will go into more specific details on how to approach realization and application, but regardless of the style, how it can be applied can largely be looked at in two ways.

First, as a core expectation and feature of the project, which requires a clear style guide, breakdown of tech needs and team structure in order to get project leadership's full support. This is likely tied to pushing a single axis further than the above examples: an especially unique art vision, a team that is especially skilled in a specific style of animation, a desire to realize a new technology or a project desire to find every way possible to differentiate from competitors in a competitive genre. Regardless of the reason, if the animation style is defined as a core expectation, defining the style guide for this will need to be a top priority so that the team can create a cohesive realization of the style at full production and scale. And the needs can be identified and clarified as early as possible.

The other approach to style is to think of it as an additional layer to the animation vision that can be allowed to grow organically or applied after the fact as part of a polish phase. To let it grow organically throughout pre-production, what is required is a general, lightly defined direction based on all of the investigations done around expectations, needs and team structure. The value here is that it affords the most flexibility for upstream iteration and the ability to restrain or push the style based on where the project naturally leads. The danger is that the style can become a patchwork of aesthetic choices or lack the immediate appeal a strongly defined style can afford.

The other side of this approach is to think of the style as something that can be applied in a final polish stage, either by hand, rendering techniques or procedural treatments. This can allow for the style work to be decoupled from proving out other project needs, which can give it the space required to be defined. But this then runs the risk of not working out or being deprioritized. Regardless of using this approach as something that grows organically or as a future layer, there needs to be an understanding that this could be cut and the animation vision and project needs would still be met.

With that in mind, let us look at different categories of style, how they fit into the graph, and how style can influence, communicate and drive the needs of the project and the overall animation vision.

REALISM

While Realism is on one end of an axis, it is worthwhile expanding the area of this style to include a bit more of the chart. How large of a section to include is subjective and possibly a worthwhile exercise to have amongst your art and animation team. But moving forward, this is what I mean when I speak of realism as a style (Figure 7.7).

Ultimately, the core of the style is to be almost entirely informed by what is natural in terms of timing, posing and motion. The majority of AA and AAA games generally fall within this category. It offers the most flexibility in terms of the tools available (keyframe, capture and procedural) and can be the most straightforward to direct because we, as humans, are all experts on what looks and feels 'real.' As such, it is likely that the constraints of tech, time and people will influence where in the box of realism your project will sit.

If the intent of the project is to push for hyper-realism, as far to the right of the line as possible, then make sure the studio and project leadership are aware of what they are signing up for. Pushing beyond the currently established limit on any axis can be challenging, but hyper-realism

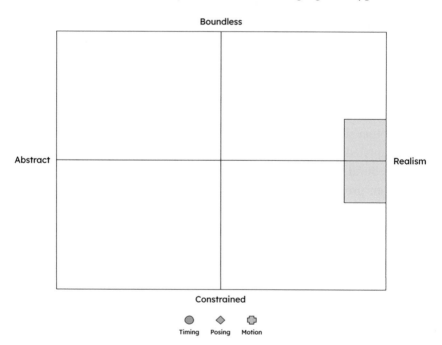

FIGURE 7.7 The purple box on the right side of the chart shows the area I am considering as realism.

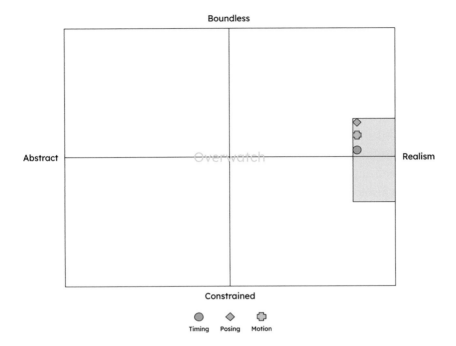

FIGURE 7.8 A coordinate graph used to plot the elements of style for *Overwatch*.

is an ever-advancing technological arms race. It can be exciting to be at the forefront of new technologies, pushing the boundaries beyond what people have seen before. But that requires a mix of experienced people in both art and tech, which requires time, money and trust.

It is also worthwhile to note that of the four example games, the one representing this group, *The Last of Us 2*, had the elements the closest together. This shows that if you want to hit this mark and stand out, the vision and aim need to be incredibly precise. Even games that people would consider more stylized, like Overwatch with pushed poses, smear frames and snappy timing, would still fit within this box. Which is to say, pushing even towards the edges of this box can help your animation style stand out (Figure 7.8).

If the project's intent is to deliver a standout animation style within this box, attaching the key technology, tools and training to the core features can help. Those features are less likely to be cut and more likely to be prioritized, making the investment in the needs of the style a clear benefit to the project. Just keep in mind that those features are also the most likely to have a lot of cross-discipline focus and iteration, which can impact the speed and requirements of the technology in both positive and frustrating ways. It may be required for specific deadlines, which can add pressure to deliver an unknown creative and technological endeavor on an unnatural timeline. Or the feature the style needs to support changes enough that how it needs to be applied requires rework at a foundational level to support, which again results in an unnatural timeline. For the inverse, attaching more risky style needs to novelty features can be both good and bad, as it is less likely to get much focus beyond those directly invested in the feature. This means those passionate about inclusion can push on it at their own speed, and it can come online at almost any time during the project. But that also means it can be cut at any time during project development if something with a higher need or priority demands the support.

When approaching realism with a more organic approach, establishing the direction of emotional traits or physical movement elements will be key. That direction will provide consistency in the breadth and depth of where inspiration can be found to help set the performances apart from other experiences with a similar style. Even within the bounds of realism, humans are capable of an incredible range of motion and performance. The choices available to animators and actors within a realistic style do not need to ever be considered generic, basic or vanilla. Regardless of style, remember that acting is *'an action in pursuit of an objective to overcome an obstacle.'* Keeping that in mind will always make a performance feel alive and inspired within a highly competitive and established style like realism.

As the foundation of the project and its workflows becomes more solid, you can then more specifically plot the style elements within the box that most naturally fit the current trajectory and capacity afforded to the team. And see where a little push in any direction can help the style stand out a bit more.

Realism, while crowded, still offers a lot of opportunities for growth and exploration. As humans, we are all experts on what is real and believable, and we have not yet reached the end of the realism axis. The push to realize that in a digital, interactive medium still has a long way to go, in both substantial and incremental ways. As the tools and technology continue to evolve to reduce the scope and technical hurdles of creating fully realistic movement, the opportunities for realizing more natural character performances will also grow. And that is something actors have continued to both chase and define in an effort to consistently find and communicate in a way that honestly connects with the character and audience.[1] Adding a layer of interactivity there almost certainly makes it both easier and harder for the future of realism in games.

LIMITED

This pertains to a style that is purposefully constrained in how it uses time, pose and/or motion. Think of styles that are very pose-to-pose, with minimal motion between the poses. Or characters and objects that are often greatly simplified in shape or detail. More often than not, the most common tools in the case of limited styles are likely either keyframe or procedural, as those most naturally suit themselves to a limited style. But like realism, do not let the name fool you into falling into uninspired choices when it comes to the animation vision and a character's performance. With fewer frames, the choices you make for each can become even more important, as those frames need to carry the appeal of the performance. Again, the focus on traits and motion elements can help establish a clear direction on what makes each character stand out within a style with more constraints. This also makes the importance of workflows that allow for quick posing, implementation and iteration one of the most valuable areas you can invest in, in terms of technology. This will allow you to spend more time on the variety or polish of the actions and poses powering the performance.

There is a long history of limited animation techniques that push forward the possibility of style by providing a new approach towards realizing appealing characters and performances. UPA,[2] anime and even the earliest generations of games that employed pixel art and then 3D have all found creative success within the constraints of limited animation elements. Many of the most classic game characters, poses and actions have become iconic and persisted, even as the animation itself has pushed beyond the original limited style (Figure 7.9).

The tension that comes from constraints removing some traditional options can be of great creative inspiration if given the opportunity to

FIGURE 7.9 Mario's iconic jump pose has persisted, building upon the original constraints of posing and motion.

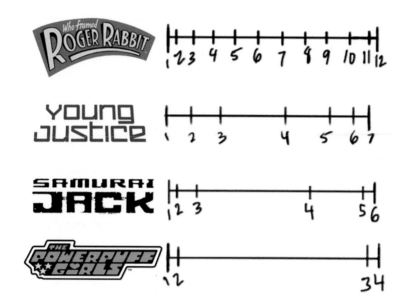

FIGURE 7.10 The timing charts that define the general approach each show or film takes in terms of the spacing of their key frames for most actions.

commit to it. Timing is a perfect example of this. Here you can see examples of how defining specific timing charts for a project can make it immediately look and feel different from others (Figure 7.10).

Roger Rabbit, being entirely on ones, allows for boundless opportunities in terms of timing, as every frame is controlled by the animator. But for the *Powerpuff Girls*, or anything that is incredibly pose-to-pose, the constraints around the timing create an incredibly distinct and consistent style of timing for each action. When applying both of those to the graph, it would look like this (Figure 7.11).

With this in mind, let us return to *Overwatch*. What would that look like if we moved the timing to be more constrained? (Figure 7.12)

By only moving one style element towards the abstract and adding constraints, it would make for a more stylized vision for the animation. Imagine everything about the existing animation in the game, but with the timing and spacing matching that of *Powerpuff Girls*. How would you approach this? Would you rely on more smear frames to convey the broader actions, similar to how much they are used in *The Dover Boys*[3]? Would that then also pull your motion element closer to abstract? How would this work for a game that is exclusively online where this style

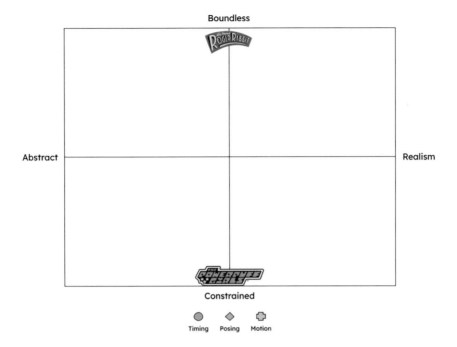

FIGURE 7.11 A coordinate graph used to plot the style of timing for *Roger Rabbit* and *Powerpuff Girls*.

of timing could come across as lags or frame rate issues? Realizing this would certainly require effort in hitting quality and consistency needs, which would then force conversations similar to realism in how best to find the support required. As you discuss all of this, it may be clear that an approach like this to the style is pushed too far, but you can see how somewhere between this and the existing timing style would land in a more stop-motion aesthetic, along the lines of *Arcane*. And even by having this conversation, you can establish that the projects and aesthetics people see as 'stylized' can be pushed even further by adding constraints to the style elements.

The sooner you can understand and embrace the constraints, the more likely you are to communicate the creative intent in a way that is both clear and appealing.

EXAGGERATED

The classical definition of exaggeration, as written in *The Illusion of Life*,[4] is to remain true to reality, just presenting it in a wilder, more extreme form.

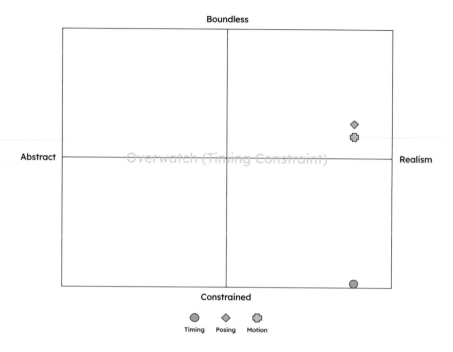

FIGURE 7.12 A coordinate graph used to plot the elements of style for *Overwatch*, but timing is moved to being fully constrained.

This means anytime you chart an element towards the abstract and boundless, and in some cases, even constrained, you are moving towards an exaggerated style. This is how many of those limited styles, such as UPA, anime and stop-motion, can be both limited and exaggerated in their styles. But if limited is, generally speaking, the bottom half of the style graph, most people are likely to think of exaggerated as being the top half of the style graph. It is hard not to be intrigued by the more open possibility space of the boundless and abstract. *Cuphead* immediately captured public attention, based in large part by leaning directly into one area of the exaggerated style space. This is without a doubt an area with a lot of opportunity to explore. But that can also make it incredibly difficult to establish and realize any consistency in terms of a collaborative creation (Figure 7.13).

Hand-drawn animation is almost immediately best suited when approaching a more exaggerated style. By the nature of the tools, there are fewer constraints to bound the possibility space. Unlike 3d, there is no rig or control required to abstract the form during the motions. There are no additional blend shapes or models required to create a unique expression

FIGURE 7.13 Screenshots from *Cuphead* showing a flower character turn their head into a Gatling gun to fire projectiles.

or form. If the inspiration strikes to turn the character into a rocket ship during a dashing motion, there is nothing technically stopping that from happening. But to realize that in 3d would require the support of multiple disciplines across art and tech. Which means exaggeration as a novelty or rejection of realism, as often employed in cartoons, becomes exponentially more expensive and difficult in a 3d space.

That is not to say it is not worth it to replicate in 3d; it just takes forethought and planning to accomplish. However, the results can almost immediately make the style stand out from other similar games in a genre. And if you attach the style to the core player experience, it can even inspire new verbs, actions and forms of interactivity to incorporate into the design.

And while it is unlikely the first tool people think of in terms of exaggeration, capture can be of use here. Inherently exaggerated methods of movement like rhythmic gymnastics, contortionists and symbolic or expressionistic acting will allow you to capture people who have trained their bodies for exaggerated motions and actions. This will be a great starting point for establishing a ground truth to always start from, with each animator then further exaggerating the motion in their own way. Add in elements of wire work, jump boards and other stage rigging elements, and suddenly you can have some incredibly exaggerated performances with the benefit of collaborating with experts in a unique field of movement. You may be working with a ballet dancer, who when presented with an action to close the door behind them while carrying an object, results in an arabesque position after effortlessly kicking their leg back and up to close the door. While this is entirely a realistic action and available within the realm of realism, the very nature of the theatricality of ballet makes it ripe to fully lean into when employing a more exaggerated style.

Another tool that can suit the exaggerated style well is procedural methods. While a lot of applications see it used in a more constrained manner, using it as a layer of reactive physics,[5] there is just as much an opportunity to tune the values to exaggerate reality. Most applications of this are likely going to lead to more comical uses, such as extra-floppy ragdoll, but thinking of physics between tense and loose is very similar to constrained and boundless. *Gang Beasts* and *Rain World* are both wonderful examples of games that use procedural animation to bring expressive characters and motions to life (Figure 7.14).

FIGURE 7.14   A screenshot from *Rain World*.

EXPERIMENTAL

This speaks to styles that break convention or expectations around how time, pose or motion believably behave. This pushes beyond the axis or lives in the corners of the abstract, constrained and boundless. But it does not require all three of the style elements to be at those extremes. By the very nature of being experimental, it is impossible to fully convey the potential here. But there are a couple of examples that have resonated with me that can also highlight to you what more can be out there.

Let's first return to *140*, the example for abstract in the style coordinate graph. Specifically, take note of the motion element in the bottom left corner.

The avatar in *140* is a series of shapes, depending on the state you are in. When you are idle, you are a square. When you move left or right, you are a circle. When you jump, you are a triangle. All motion is a linear blend between these actions. Save for the moving jump, which maintains the shape of a triangle but adds some rotation to infer the connection to the left-right movement of being a circle. The motions are both exceptionally abstract and constrained. But the sensation of movement FEELS correct. If we return to the definition of art here, *'an idea communicated with creative intent'*, the animation in this game perfectly demonstrates that in an abstract and constrained way. And the reason it is successful is because the intent is so clear. And as humans, we cannot help but impose context on anything we feel is conveyed with intent. Even with almost every possible element of context or intent stripped away, an audience will lean in when given something so clearly intentional.

Let us now look towards the other side of the coordinate graph, which is where we can often find the works of Jan Švankmajer. Using a mix of live action, pixilation[6] and stop-motion, Jan is able to immediately leverage the expectations of realism to ultimately subvert those expectations in surreal ways. For instance, here are a couple of screen shots from one of his shorts, *Food* (Figure 7.15).

Posing, timing and motion generally start on the right side of the graph, but from there they can fluctuate their position on the style graph all throughout one of Jan's shorts. By that very nature, it can be hard to translate this into a coherent or cohesive vision or direction. But the use of pixilation overlaps, influences and mimics elements of earlier generations of game animation in ways that should be immediately obvious. *Mortal Kombat* is essentially pixilation. *Clayfighter* took the same process but used stop-motion techniques instead of humans. Full-motion video (FMV) has been used in games for even longer. Which is all to say, there

FIGURE 7.15 Screenshots from *Food* by Jan Švankmajer.

is nothing stopping us from having an interactive Jan Švankmajer-style experience. And while mimicry is not inherently experimental, it can at least be a wonderful catalyst for breaking out of established norms.

Creativity and style are like an ocean. It is a vast mix of the known and unknown. The experience of setting off prepared to sail is a wildly different adventure from the one you would have if you were dropped off in the middle of the ocean on a raft. While people and teams may think what they want is to create with limitless options, that is actually like dropping them into the middle of the ocean with only the clothes on their back. Some people may enjoy that unique challenge, but most are looking for a general destination or goal so that they can enjoy their creative journey with confidence that they are not going to get lost. All of the focus on expectations, needs and vision has been to give them a reliable compass, map and vessel when they find themselves in the creative ocean. Which means the next step is to get them to all paddle in the same direction.

NOTES

1 This is yet another reason to read Isaac Butler's *The Method: How the Twentieth Century Learned to Act*.

2 The United Productions of America expertly show how constraints can unlock new creative opportunities when done with intent. I highly recommend watching *The World of UPA* on The Royal Ocean Film Society's Youtube channel.

3 You can rather easily watch *The Dover Boys* online thanks to it being part of the public domain. It pushes the use of limited animation and smear frames to a level that you can see still influencing modern animation styles.

4 It seems almost silly to reference Frank Thomas & Ollie Johnston's *The Illusion of Life: Disney Animation* again, as anyone reading this almost certainly must have read that. But it is a classic for a reason, and if any animation book demands being in the reference notes more than once, it is this.

5 As discussed in Chapter 3, Michael Mach's 2017 GDC talk *Physics Animation in Uncharted 4: A Thief's End* is a great entry point to see how procedural methods can be layered on top of existing animations.

6 One of the best ways to get someone to experience the craft of animating without needing to know how to draw or learn new technology is through pixelation. By using any camera, you can have people act out a motion or scene one frame and picture at a time. A great breakdown of the practice and history of the method can be found on the studiobinder blog titled *Pixilation Animation – Definition, Examples and Techniques*.

CHAPTER 8

Communicating the Vision

E VERYTHING UP TO THIS point has been about understanding the ideas that need to be communicated and defining the creative intent around how they can be communicated. But like with all art, you cannot take the communication of thought and creative intent for granted. There is a wealth of ideas and knowledge you should now understand and have available to you. Within your head and scattered across your own series of videos, documents and sketches is the animation vision of the project. Now is the time to bring all of that together in a way that it can be easily shared and understood by everyone, which will help realize the vision. Lucky for us, it has been proven that animation is an inherently powerful tool for learning and retention.[1] Especially when you apply the same care to understanding and communicating the creative intent as you would in any other part of the craft.

STYLE AND TONE VIDEO

At this point, you will likely have a number of reference videos, animation tests and visualization elements around performance, style, competitive examples and other pieces that inspire the animation vision. The style and tone video is a great way to tie all of the elements together and show the full possibility space available. For the *Dragon Age* style and tone video,[2] the intent was to show the breadth of the style and tone available to the team

DOI: 10.1201/9781003356196-8

to help inform early tests and pre-production work. This was the video to show new and potential team members to get them excited about how far we could push the style and tone of animation. Which meant realizing this video required the same attention to the art and craft as expected by any other part of the creative process.

Communicating an Idea (Animation Vision) with Creative Intent (Style and Tone)

The vision of the game was to still be grounded and believable, but to push to the edges of realism. In terms of style, including each element (timing, posing and motion) in the corner of each clip is incredibly valuable in letting people know what they should specifically be taking from the clip. In the case of a *Spider-verse* clip, it is valuable to not have timing on there so that people understand that the more constrained, stop-motion style of timing is not an element to explore or incorporate. Having spent time understanding the elements of style before making this will make it much easier to research and select the appropriate clips to use. It also allows you to purposefully search out and work to include reference points beyond what might be expected. If they don't ultimately fit, having the style elements as guide posts should help to keep you honest (Figure 8.1).

FIGURE 8.1 A screen shot from Jason Hendrich's *Shadow Crush*, a clip of which was used as one example to convey the posing and motion opportunities available to the animation team, even when the rendering style isn't the same.

When it comes to conveying the tone, it is good to look back on the project's needs and vision. The high-level animation vision for *Dragon Age*, as informed by the project vision, was to *Boldly Reflect Choice and Intent*. This meant 'bold' was the tone that needed to be conveyed here. To do this, I created different titles with which to group together different clips to establish a connection related to different areas of focus within the team.

- *Bold Lines of Action*

- *Bold Actions*

- *Bold Personalities*

- *Bold Creatures*

Having these groups both informs and is informed by the reference clips that match the tone of the game. One of the objectives of the project was to fully embrace the breadth of tone beyond the outward image of dark, violent fantasy. Knowing that initial perceptions of the tone tend towards dramatic high fantasy, it became important to push against the edges of that perception to find the limits of what could be accepted. This meant including references to the performance and personality defined in the previous chapters that would help to most push the edges of what a complete adoption of 'bold' would be within an established and grounded fantasy setting. Starting the video by showing more bold tone choices in terms of accepted areas of what people expect from animation, posing (Bold Lines of Action) and motion (Bold Actions), allowed the viewer to open up to the possibility space when pushing the tone in terms of performance (Bold Personalities) and physicality (Bold Creatures), which can require more cross disciplinary support and realization.

Because the overall art and creative style of the project were being refreshed, I chose to include clips from life and film when conveying style and tone instead of creating specific animations to convey everything. I specifically didn't want to include legacy models or characters, as those could influence people's perception of how the previous characters moved or performed. For a similar reason, I also chose not to include other games as references here. There are a number of constraints and perceptions that come attached to using other games as references, above and beyond the animation itself. Understanding that constraints are one axis on the style graph means that you need to be conscious of including constraints here that would be perceived beyond those intended in the style. Life and animated films naturally have fewer unintentional constraints in terms of style, so they carry with them less baggage in terms of style constraints.

In terms of the length of this video, 2–3 minutes is likely the sweet spot. The video I made was closer to 4 minutes, which was certainly pushing it. However, the length of videos will very much depend on the audience and how the video is primarily presented, which will be discussed further in this chapter. So, think of the 2- to 3-minute mark as a good goal to initially aim for as you force yourself to only include the most impactful and necessary clips.

VISUAL TARGET VIDEO

The visual target video is meant to represent what the final game and/or experience will look like.[3] The goal is to be able to show with full clarity what the needs and expectations are in terms of feature realization and quality bar without needing to wait the months or years that may be required to get specific features or elements of the project to a similar state. Much like the Competitive Analysis video discussed in Chapter 4, the Visual Target video can inform specific decisions and needs in terms of tech and support. If the Competitive Analysis video is especially valuable in the earliest R&D or conceptual stages of development, the Visual Target video is valuable as a requirement in the early or mid-Pre-Production stages. It allows the team to further inform the priorities that came from the Competitive Analysis tech breakdown as well as realize portions of the animation vision that are best seen in practice to be understood and validated. But the specifics of what is needed, how best to realize this and the value it will bring very much depend on several different factors unique to your project.

New Experience

If this is an entirely new project with new characters, world, ideas and intent, then this video can be a powerful way to align everyone on how to specifically realize the vision. There are generally two approaches here. A narrative-focused cinematic and/or a representation of what the final gameplay will look like. Both have inherent value but slightly different risks and rewards.

In terms of a narrative cinematic, this allows the team to fully realize the narrative, visual and audio presentation of the project. And ideally inform or define the cinematic pipeline for the game, if one is required. Focusing on a narrative cinematic removes some complexity around trying to define design and tech that is likely undergoing regular exploration and iteration, which can make for fewer vision holders during the creation and approval of the video. Another benefit of making this is that it can often double as an announcement trailer for the project, as it is specifically meant to convey the tone and style of the world and characters. Which means the final creation doubles as both a realization target and a piece of marketing.

The trade-off of a narrative cinematic is that you will have several of the most senior and experienced members of the team involved in this as their top priority. Which can take away from direct feature support as well as create some hacks or band-aids that won't scale well. This can be mitigated by working with an external team, which can also help to establish the process of working with external partners. The trade-off there is that you will be establishing the execution of the vision with external partners, which can take longer due to the nature of external collaboration. And it establishes expertise within an external team as opposed to the internal team. Which means the integration and reliance of that external team should become a priority for the project so that the expertise is not immediately lost after the cinematic wraps.

In terms of a representative gameplay cinematic, this is especially valuable if there is a need to visualize gameplay needs for the team to aspire towards. This has all the complexity of a narrative cinematic trailer but also includes collaboration with design, tech, UI and UX to realize and present a fuller player experience. This means it becomes especially important to clearly define the exact features and elements that need to be defined, as iteration and feedback here can easily become stuck in a loop of conflicting needs, priorities and dependencies. This can make it a natural test bed for defining clear production and approval processes, discussed in more depth in Chapters 9 and 10.

Things to keep in mind here are that this is very likely going to require work that will not be able to be directly used outside of this video. Bits and pieces might translate in terms of individual animations, models and cinematic tech. But largely, this video exists to inform the team of how the game is meant to look and play. This makes the audience largely an internal one, though it is important to clarify if the priority is to inform the team members making the project or the investors funding the project. The internal team is more likely to have 'dev goggles' and read between the lines in terms of certain elements that aren't as fully realized or polished as others. If the priority is to sell investors securing or unlocking additional funding, then the priority is likely to make every part consistently polished and realized. It is also important to understand if this is ever intended to be released as a marketing trailer. Generally, this approach can backfire for developers, as features and elements continue to iterate after the video as they become realized in the game and need to be adjusted once they need to run through the actual systems and tech, both runtime and dcc.

Regardless of the method, both can be powerful tools to clarify the vision of a new project for a team and help point them all in a unified direction. But due to the number of unknowns, this should be considered a substantial part of early pre-production, as it will require a lot of leadership and experienced members of the team to deliver.

New Genre

If this is a new genre, different from those previously made by an established team or studio, then a visual target video can also be incredibly valuable. Almost all genres of games have established expectations and requirements that each team member can perceive differently. This is where the visual target can help clarify which elements of the genre are being included, subverted or ignored.

The more different a core aspect of a genre is from the previous experience of the team, the higher the priority should be to realize the experience. If it has been a gameplay-focused team and now there is an expectation of narrative, a narrative cinematic trailer can be helpful in assembling the people and processes needed to work through the tone and voice of the narrative. The needs and expectations of movement and combat for a 3rd-person single-player, turn-based action rpg are different from those of a 3rd-person multiplayer looter shooter. Being able to visibly align across disciplines on those earlier rather than later is incredibly beneficial in the amount of effort required to fully realize that.

The biggest difference here is that there is most likely an existing foundation of tech, workflows and experience to build upon. This can be both good and bad. Some of the foundations will be able to transfer more easily than others. A fair amount of this should already be understood from the investigation into tech needs in Chapter 4. This means it may be possible to realize some or all parts of the visual target video in the engine faster than if you were to make it entirely cinematic. How much will depend on the unique situation of your project, tech and team. But it is very much worth defining early on when discussing how to best create the video.

New Features

It may be that instead of needing to define the core vision and experience for the project, there are some specific features that need to be realized. All of the same pros and cons in terms of approach to a wholly new experience or genre are the same here, but applied to a smaller, more focused need. But beyond proving out the more specific need, it is important to keep in mind that beyond the individual feature(s), you should also consider how it connects to the larger experience. There are some valuable questions to ask when considering how best to approach realization.

- *How is it triggered? (Player input, trigger volume in the environment, other players, npc, etc.)*

- *Where is it triggered? (In gameplay, in UI, during a cinematic, etc.)*

- *How does it transition to other aspects of the game? (Seamlessly to other features, to a UI menu, etc.)*

Being able to answer these will help you understand the best tools to use to visualize the feature and how best to implement it into an existing foundation to get a sense of how it connects to and flows with the larger player experience. It will also help you to understand if this video is best suited to be shown outside of the game or something that is triggered in the game. Having it triggered in the game can be especially valuable for narrative-focused features, as it can help to give a general sense of the pacing as part of the realization.

New Style or Tone

What is most likely needed here is a video to sell people a style or tone that is outside of what the team has done before. There could be reservations around both the fit of the new aesthetics and the team's ability to deliver on something new and different. Understanding which of these is the priority is important. If it is around the team's ability to hit on a new style or tone, make sure you are setting them up for the best chance at success. This means that defining as part of the pre-production process requires a clear vision, time to invest in any required research, testing, tool support, training and mentorship to deliver on the new style and tone. While that is happening, work with the project leadership to identify opportunities to prove out the new style and tone in an area of the game that would most benefit from the realization of the style and tone, while providing as little friction as possible in terms of new tech or cross-disciplinary dependencies. This is likely secondary or tertiary features like character select screens, emotes and fidgets, or non-critical cinematics or scripted events.

If the team's ability isn't in question, then it is likely less about proving quality and more about proving how the new style or tone fits within the larger project vision. If this is the case, choosing whichever tools the team has available to quickly show how the style and tone fit is the priority. In the case of *Dragon Age*, the idea of using modern, hip-hop style dance moves for magic casting was something people had reservations about. So instead of creating an incredibly polished cinematic simulation of battle, it made more sense to show the act of using dance movements as a way of intentionally casting magic. This started by using the dance magic movement elements vision video[4] to inform the casting, direction and performances of the dancers on the mocap stage. The editing together the video from that shoot, along with the roughly timed mocap data applied to input for movement and attacks, made for a quick and clear realization video. Seeing this with the animation in an even rough state was enough to convince people that the new style and tone of magic casting fit the project vision.

New Tech

It may be that a substantial tech investment into a new feature is required, and while the high-level intent is clear, as are the foundational tech needs, what is less clear is what the final product is meant to look like. This is where a visual target video is incredibly valuable, as it allows everyone to see what the end result should look like. As well as prioritize specific workflows and tools to support the team members using the tech.

In some instances, the new tech need may already exist in another toolset, be it a dcc or public engine. If that is the case, it may be easier to create a video or prototype directly from that toolset. Just be mindful of licenses and copyrights in terms of how closely the code and tools replicate an existing set of tools or tech.

Also, be mindful of the fact that the customers for this video are the team members building the tech and those that will be primarily focused on using the tech. So it is important to establish with them the specific needs and questions that need to be addressed by this video.

New Team

Another prime opportunity to make a visual target video is when you are working on a team that is largely comprised of new team members. Teams find success through trust and strong communication, which is something a visual target video can help foster. The creation of it should have clearly defined delivery goals, a controlled amount of complexity and cross-disciplinary dependencies that ultimately result in a final product that gives the team confidence and trust in their abilities and the project's vision.

DIFFERENT AUDIENCES

We have touched on this a bit up to this point, but now that you have assembled a wealth of videos, references and vision documents, it is important to start thinking about how best to share the vision as a whole. Communicating a total vision is an art form, like telling a story. This means you need to be intentional about how you establish the elements of the vision, the pacing at which you discuss each element and how you connect them all together with the high-level vision as a whole. The variable to all of this is that different audiences will have different levels of expertise or understanding of animation and all of the specific elements of the vision to be discussed. This means you will want to adjust what and how you share the animation vision to best cater to the different audiences involved. The main audiences are usually the animation team, the leadership team, the entire project team and a general audience. Let us look at how best to communicate the animation vision to each other.

Animation Team

The animation team is obviously knowledgeable about the craft of animation, so everything you have gathered is most likely ready to be presented in its current form without any major edits to the materials. The trick here is organizing everything into a clear-to-follow format, as opposed to a shotgun blast of information. To do this, I like to make a slide deck that breaks down the vision across all major areas of the project and an organized wiki that further expands each of those areas.

For the slide deck, it is worthwhile to make it match the overall style and tone of the project. Ideally, there is a project slide template that has already been created by someone on the team when pitching the project. If not, then it is worth working with art, UI and marketing leadership to make sure you have access to all the visual elements required to make this look as on brand as possible. You want access to the most up-to-date concept art, fonts, logos and music that are being used to represent and sell the project. This will help you immediately establish and convey the animation vision as part of the larger project vision. As well as leverage the strength of your teammates to create an appealing presentation. First impressions matter when communicating a vision. And nothing undercuts a vision quite like a generic PowerPoint template.

With the visual style of the deck established, now comes laying out the high-level beats of the presentation. Each project will likely require some specific adjustments, but using everything discussed up to this point, a good place to start is:

- *High-Level Vision Tagline*
  - *Project and Animation (Chapter 2)*

- *Vision Teaser Video*
  - *30 seconds of various clips to give a taste of the vision*

- *Goals*
  - *Project and Team Expectations (Chapter 1)*

- *Features*
  - *Competitive Analysis Video (Chapter 4)*

- *Performance and Movement Vision*
  - *Personality and Movement Element Videos (Chapter 6)*

- *Style and Tone*

  - *Style and Tone Video (Chapter 7)*

- *Quality Targets*

  - *Visual Target Videos (Above)*

- *Obstacles*

  - *Tech Needs (Chapter 4)*

- *Timeline*

  - *Current stage of development and estimated ship date*

- *Team Structure*

  - *Team Structure Chart (Chapter 5)*

When it comes to conveying the vision as it applies to every feature and character, it is best to choose one area as a representation of the intent and process that will then be applied to defining every other feature and character in the game. In the instance of *Dragon Age*, the focus of the vision deck was on the player character in order to deep dive into the intent applied to defining their personality trait video, faction movement elements, style and tone, and how that related to combat, exploration, cinematics and conversations. Once everything was discussed in terms of the player character, another short video was cut together showing clips of personality trait videos for important non-player characters, faction movement element videos for enemy characters and world animation references to show how the intent behind the vision could be applied to all aspects of the project. And to give a sense of the full possibility space with which to draw from and apply all manners of different references.

Once you have these elements together, consider this your first pass. Run through the presentation a few times, talking aloud to yourself. This will force you to be able to clearly communicate the vision in words. Areas that don't seem to flow well or that you find yourself stumbling through are great indicators that you need to spend some more time grasping. It could be that what you are trying to explain is too complex or too vague. It could be that there is a missing piece required to connect everything together. Think of this vision deck like a puzzle. See what pieces you have left, which areas of the puzzle are missing a piece, and see if they fit. If not, then discard or adjust the pieces that don't fit for ones that will. It doesn't matter how perfect each puzzle piece looks on its own if it doesn't fit into the larger picture.

After you have run through the presentation enough times that you are comfortable with it, choose a few members of the team that you know will be honest with you, ideally covering the art and tech spectrum, and present the vision to them. As you are presenting, take notice of which areas they seem to especially engage with and which areas they seem to tune out. You are also likely to notice, when presenting to others, which areas seem to drag on or are rushed. Once you finish, ask them for feedback on any areas of the vision that remain unclear, elements that are missing or anything in general that feels out of place. Compare their answers to your mental notes to see where there is overlap between your perception and their reception. Make the necessary adjustments and choose some new team members to present it to. Compare their feedback to the original feedback, and then rinse and repeat until you have a presentation that you are confident with. At which point, present it to the entire animation team, leaving time for discussion. As this has been an ongoing and collaborative effort, there are likely already elements of the vision that have evolved or adjusted beyond what people may have seen or contributed to. This is the moment to align everyone on the team with the actual vision. And any areas that need further explanation or clarification at this point are best expanded on through a wiki, which can more easily be a living document for the vision.

Once you have your vision deck complete, get to work on structuring confluence, one note or some other wiki-style resource the project uses as its source of truth. This is where you and everyone on the team can document in more detail the vision and processes of animation on the project. Try to structure it in a way that builds upon the flow of the presentation deck but can naturally support the full team now contributing to the realization of the vision. I like to use the following format:

- *01. Animation Vision*
  - *Link to the vision presentation*
  - *Create pages for each section of the presentation that can be expanded upon with more references to address lingering questions*

- *02. Animation Production Practices*
  - *Completion Standards (Chapter 9)*
  - *Comparative Targets (Chapter 9)*
  - *Tracking Sheets (Chapter 9)*
  - *Review and Approval Process (Chapter 10)*

- *03. Animation Team*
  - *Team Structure (Chapter 5)*
  - *Interests and Values (Chapter 12)*

- *04. Animation Tech, Tools and Workflows*
  - *Tools and Pipelines (Chapter 3)*
  - *New Tech and Workflows (Chapter 4)*
  - *File Naming Conventions*
  - *Metrics (Chapter 2)*
  - *Reference Libraries (Chapter 10)*

- *05. Animation Training Resources*
  - *Videos, Books, Workshops, Career Growth (Chapter 12)*

- *06. Archive*
  - *Out-of-Date material*

This layout should provide just enough structure to let people find what they are looking for as well as where they should save their documentation and references. It can be easy for this to become both messy and out of date quickly, so it is important to assume and assign responsibility for the upkeep of this across the animation leadership team. It can be valuable to book yourself a recurring reminder or block of time each month to go through this wiki and make sure it is organized and up to date. The archive can be especially valuable as it allows you to move anything you don't want to lose, but is no longer relevant, to a section that allows it to still exist for future reference. Just make sure to append 'Out of Date' to the title of the page for anyone that may come across it through a search.

Once you have the vision presentation and the wiki established for the animation team, the direction and goals of the project should be clear to the entire animation team. Congratulations! Getting to this point is no small feat and you should now be able to speak with confidence about the totality of the animation direction for the project. Take a moment to celebrate and then it is time to make some edits to the presentation to fit other audiences beyond the animation team.

Leadership Team

When it comes to communicating your vision up and across the project, studio and publisher leadership, it is important to keep it focused on how it adds value to the high-level needs, features and vision of the project. And specifically, how the animation vision reinforces the different aspects of the game, even if it is being communicated in a way that wasn't initially expected. You want to show people where the vision is and where it is going. And everything else around how you got there can be shared if asked. Because you spent time understanding all of the needs of the project, the intent behind the vision is solid. What you want to communicate is how far beyond the expected conventions the animation vision plans to push and where there may be concerns that still need to be addressed. This allows you to prioritize finding the limits of the vision within those areas of concern. It will also show you which areas the leadership team is most excited about, which will provide opportunities for the team to build trust and goodwill for and within the project.

To do all of this, think of a version of the vision presentation that is 15–30 minutes long. To start with, you can likely pair down the original deck into one that only includes the following sections:

- *High-Level Vision Tagline*
    - *Animation (Chapter 2)*

- *Goals*
    - *Project Expectations (Chapter 1)*

- *Features*
  - *Competitive Analysis Video (Chapter 4)*

- *Style and Tone*
  - *Style and Tone Video (Chapter 7)*

- *Quality Targets*
  - *Highest Level Visual Target Videos (Above)*

- *Obstacles*
  - *Tech Needs (Chapter 4)*

- *Team Structure*
  - *Team Structure Chart (Chapter 5)*

The goal of this video is to show there is a plan and direction established, remove ambiguity around what animation will be focused on, define the support that will be required to get there and ultimately define what things are going to look like when they get there. This is the audience that you will need to turn to for cross-disciplinary support and to provide additional resources when required. This presentation should give them the confidence to trust the direction and the team to deliver on what is being presented with as few surprises as possible. And you can always link to the full presentation and confluence page for anyone who wants to get into more detail.

Project Team

The project team lives between the previous two audiences, in that you have some people that will be partnering on the execution of the vision and also others that are not going to be directly contributing to the execution but reliant on knowing what to expect. This means that you can likely start by sharing the leadership presentation while specifically highlighting links to the full presentation and wiki. That gives the sales pitch as well as the details for those that will be working in more specific areas that partner directly with animation. But it is also important to find opportunities to expand upon specific elements of the vision that might be particularly exciting, new or subversive, so that the team can better take in the vision and appreciate the intent behind it.

As an example, on *Dragon Age*, we had been working with the writing team to create personality trait videos for each of the followers so that we could better understand and unify the performances of characters across gameplay, cinematics and the world. Once the videos were created, it gave, for the first time, a chance to experience the characters beyond the written page, which was incredibly exciting. By the nature of how the videos are made to quickly define the possibility space for each character, they are naturally engaging and easy to share. While it would have been easy to simply share the location of the videos on the wiki, this felt like an opportunity to celebrate the collaborative process between narrative and animation. As well as highlight a key feature of the project and BioWare games in general, which is the player's relationship with followers. This gave birth to the idea of presenting the videos as part of a *Dragon Age Love Connection* style presentation.

This consisted of creating a slide deck with each personality trait video, starting with the player character, who would be the 'contestant.' Then each follower was presented as potential dates, using their personality video, concept art and major reference points of creative inspiration as their dating profile. We cut together an introduction-style bumper to play at the beginning to make it feel more like a game show. To celebrate the collaborative effort, it was important to present everything in collaboration as well. I dressed in my best blazer to play the host of the show, and the writer for each follower presented each video and profile as if they were trying to set up their best friend on a blind date. To maximize attendance by the team, we made this an end-of-day event where we supplied 80s dating show-themed refreshments, like neon iced heart cookies, to help further establish and sell the tone of the presentation. Because the videos are short by nature, the presentation itself only took 15–20 minutes. Which allowed for a significant amount of remaining time for everyone to ask the narrative team questions about each character and how relationships in general were intended to work on the game. While this may seem extravagant and a silly way to convey a direction, opportunities like this create powerful moments to build trust and camaraderie amongst the team. And at that is the fuel that powers the vehicle, which everyone is collaboratively navigating together.

General Audience

This group entails a variety of audiences. The project's core fanbase. People who have never heard of your project before. External reviewers. Other game developers at a conference. In almost every case here, there is a good chance marketing and/or community managers will be involved. Which means the specifics of what you can share and when you can share it are a lot more controlled. In these cases, having all of the above elements on hand will help in being able to provide examples of what is available to be shared. Especially anything involved in the realization process is valuable, as it shows different steps of the process that can be adapted to the larger marketing needs. It can also be helpful to keep at hand any screenshots or example videos demonstrating visual targets or fully realized elements. This way, you can either help the marketing team by providing quality examples from the get-go or, at the very least, inform them of areas and opportunities that exist to be shared. The timetables and deadlines of these rarely overlap with production deadlines. And there is no guarantee you will be involved in the marketing or community process at all. But it is better to be prepared and show interest and value earlier than later, if that is something you are interested in.

With all of this established, the focus of the animation direction on the project can move from defining the intent behind the vision to now focusing on its execution.

NOTES

1 The popularity and benefits of using animation to educate technical concepts was specifically researched during World War II through The Air Forces Psychological Test Film Unit. (Hubley, John and Schwartz, Zachary. *Animation Learns a New Language.* Hollywood Quarterly, Vol. 1, No. 4 (July 1946) pp 360–363.) It is worth noting that the overlap of animated military films equally afforded new studios, directors and styles to grow, like UPA, as discussed in that article. But they also further leveraged a history of racist stereotypes in animation, which provides another good reason to read Nicholas Sammond's *Birth of an Industry: Blackface Minstrelsy and the Rise of American Animation* (2015). Understanding the full history of the craft you are directing is invaluable and necessary when communicating intent.

2 You can find the referenced tone and style video as part of the supplemental package on the book's website. It is titled Video_StyleTone. As with all of the reference material or documentation included, this should be seen as a moment of time in the development process and not an expectation of

1:1 reality. Early vision direction, such as this, should be seen as someone pointing to a location in the distance and depending on the path between where you are and where you are pointing, the path will almost certainly need to wind and adjust as you learn more along the way.

3 Like in Chapter 4, the best place to see examples of target footage is Jonathan Cooper's *The Target Game Footage* post on GameAnim.com.

4 You can find the referenced movement elements video as part of the supplemental package on the book's website. It is titled Video_Movement Elements_DanceMage.

CHAPTER 9

Defining Quality

Q UALITY IS A UNIVERSAL goal and a sign of success in any discipline or craft. Taking pride in one's work is something often instilled and celebrated during the training of a skillset, and there is something inherently clear and tangible in striving for the highest quality possible in whatever we create. No matter the task or creation, the ability to make something of higher quality is always available as a goal. It is also a default indication of growth and advancement in a craft. And to people outside of a specific craft, often the work is only commented on if it is perceived to be of especially high or low quality. All of this is to say that there is a lot of natural desire and push for the highest quality of every craft in a game.

But quality is a subjective target that often comes with a lot of assumptions, baggage from past projects and personal or discipline-focused bias. It is easy to have conversations around quality that can feel misinformed or dismissive, which can quickly cause tension between animation and other disciplines. Which can result in people or teams being boxed into conversations and perceptions entirely revolving around quality. So it is important to not only establish examples of quality but also be conscious of how to engage with these conversations.

QUALITY AND COMPLEXITY

When conversations around quality first come up, I find it can help to instead frame discussions around complexity, which is more objective. Quality ultimately comes from the complexity of the desired animation, system or scene and the time allotted for polish. The time allotted for

DOI: 10.1201/9781003356196-9

polish is often where the subjective part of the conversation lives, as that can be a variable amount of time that gives truth to the saying *'art is never finished, but abandoned.'* What more often drives quality is the desired complexity. Which means defining and agreeing to the desired complexity is the key, as that will ultimately define how much time is available and required for polish.

Several bad faith arguments can exist in this conversation, which are valuable to highlight here. But first, it is important to keep in mind that nobody on the team is actively trying to make a bad game. Everyone has different priorities and opinions on what will make for the best game possible, and it is when those don't match that you most often run into discussions around adjusting quality to ship a project or feature.

Thought-Terminating Clichés

A thought-terminating cliché is an often-repeated phrase meant to move along or end a conversation, which can come across as dismissive or insincere when used too often or meant to silence concerns.[1] There are a number of these used in everyday language, to varying degrees of success or acceptance.

- *'Let's agree to disagree'*
- *'Let's put a pin in that'*
- *'It could be worse'*
- *'Try to look on the bright side'*

None of those on their own are inherently problematic, and in the right case, they can be useful to reset a cyclical conversation, to give the time or space to redirect or discuss later in good faith. Every person, project and studio has a number of unconscious, and possibly conscious, thought-terminating clichés that they use to navigate a collaborative creative process. It is important for you to not only recognize these from others but also be aware of the ones you tend to use. I often find myself saying *'this too shall pass'* or *'such is life'* when I am presented with frustrations. In fact, a lot of times, these can be used as a way to try and remain positive in the face of adversity. But like anything, balance is required, and relentless positivity,[2] when in a leadership position, can come across as dismissive to the concerns of the team. The trick with these, when you say or hear one, is to follow up with a genuine statement showing you have heard the concern, understand the desire to move on and will make sure to follow up at the appropriate time and place.

This remains true for even more specific thought-terminating clichés, even though they may feel more personal. Common phrases here could be:

- *'No one will care about that'*

- *'Your quality bar is too high'*

- *'That isn't the game we are making'*

- *'It always comes together at the end'*

Even typing those feels more dismissive due to the more specific nature of the phrases. But the spirit is still largely the same as the more general phrases. Concerns exist, priorities are not shared, trust isn't fully established and somebody is trying to move the conversation along. Let's quickly discuss each of those root causes.

First, try to clarify the root concern for each of those statements. Especially in terms of quality, nobody is looking to put out anything that is of low quality. What they are saying is that their quality standards and tolerance are already met, and they see the quality lacking elsewhere. Which means the root concern is that too much focus on one area or feature will come at the cost of another that needs it more. In which case, it is important to know which area they are specifically concerned is going to be impacted. From there, you can then look at how each required discipline is prioritizing the features. This allows for the conversation to move to the larger experience of the project, how the different features fit together and where the complexity driving the concerns should be addressed. Which can ultimately define the best goals to collaboratively build towards, which then builds trust across the team. This is the ideal outcome of a conversation or relationship that employs frequent thought-terminating clichés. But relationships are complicated by studio structure, technical hurdles, time constraints and personal baggage.

Client and Customer Relationships

Due to the history of how games have been made and sold, there are some legacy headwinds animation directors are likely to experience. Specifically, the idea of upstream disciplines being the auteurs of game development. Some of this is natural, as earlier generations of games required more generalist skillsets, which fosters a sense of knowing how everything fits together. As games became more complex and disciplines became more specialized, those generalist roles became the connective tissue implementing the different disciplines' individual assets. Which then gave way to contractors and outsourced support as more specific work was required. This tended towards those upstream implementation and system roles seeing and touching all of the elements of a feature and the individual disciplines being more disconnected from the larger game development process. But as tools to implement have become more accessible and the nature of the player experience benefits from the expertise of specific disciplines, the idea that upstream disciplines are always best suited to carry out a project vision should not be considered a universal truth.

But that is the behind-the-scenes history of development. Thanks in large part to marketing and the history of creative productions, the public perception of upstream disciplines as the true auteurs adds significant weight to this mindset. The more public a contributor, the more associated they are with the success and value of a project. This isn't a new phenomenon, as McKay, Disney and Fleischer all celebrated their work as creative producers,[3] over properly acknowledging those doing the actual work. The through line here is clear, not only in terms of actors like Andy Serkis but also upstream leadership, as singular creative visionaries are a well-worn selling point for what are ultimately collaborative efforts. It is hard, and honestly unreasonable, to not expect that to be absorbed by anyone in that position. Which ultimately leads to two forms of creative relationships. True partnership and collaboration between disciplines. Or a customer and client relationship. Most will aspire towards partnership, but history and headwinds often point towards a customer and client relationship when push comes to shove. Often with a blanket assumption that it is the upstream team members being given the role of customer and downstream as the client.

There is nothing inherently wrong with a customer and client relationship. This has been the nature of many creative fields throughout history. But it explicitly defines a relationship where one person, the customer, is in control of what is required from the client and what is ultimately considered acceptable. This makes it more of a power structure than a true partnership. Which is to say, be aware of the actual relationship between disciplines beyond what the team structure or organization chart conveys.

Chances are that during your conversations around expectations and project needs, you already have a clear sense of these relationships and how they relate to the overall studio structure. Often, in creative collaborations, there needs to be a vision holder that drives forward the process. They are the people production partners rely upon to set cross-disciplinary directions and make decisions. The best environments are those that understand the expertise and experience of the team members, regardless of discipline, and empower the best people for the specific situation. This is becoming more common, especially for newer or smaller studios. But for a lot of larger, more established studios, there is often one or two disciplines driving the creative experience for a game, which will naturally trickle down to everyone in that discipline being seen as a customer. And in most cases, those will be upstream disciplines like design and writing. Whoever the customer is, having conversations about quality and complexity is something you should expect to have early and likely often.

Consistency

There is often a focus on defining the height of the quality bar, but even more important is the consistency of quality. Like a turd in a punch bowl, it doesn't matter how great your game looks if there is a large piece of low-quality work floating in and out of the experience. In an ideal world, there would be no lower quality work at all. Nothing but the highest quality punch. But in a production setting, with time and money constraints, it is unlikely everything can be at peak quality. Which means, instead of larger individual turds hanging out in the punch bowl, it is better to treat it like the FDA and define the maximum allocated amount of poop allowed in any cup of punch. Which this metaphor itself could probably benefit from.

In less crude terms, what you want to establish are both the peaks and valleys of quality on the project. On a scale of 1 being the lowest quality and 10 being the highest, a common pitfall is for people to always aim for a 9 or 10 at the start. What can result from this is that some elements reach between an 8–10 and several other elements fall behind at 4–6. This can make for a large swing in quality, where the peaks actually cause the drop

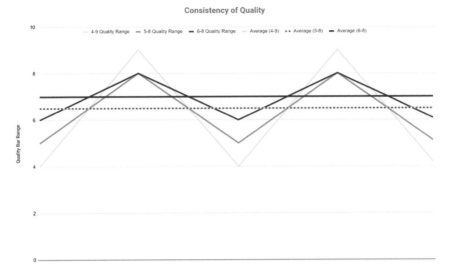

FIGURE 9.1   A line graph depicting consistency of quality between 5–8 and 4–9.

to make the lows stand out even more. For instance, let's compare a quality bar that allows for 5–8 compared to 4–9 (Figure 9.1).

As you can see, the average quality for both is around 6.5, but by lowering the high bar, you can raise the low bar. And in all honesty, lowering the high bar likely allows you to raise the low bar by 2:1, which allows for an average quality of around 7. All of which is to say, when discussions around lowering the quality bar come up, it is important to discuss how that relates to the low bar and overall consistency on the project. As people dedicated to a craft, the dream is to have a consistency bar between 8 and 10. But that isn't afforded to most productions. So it is important to be honest about the FDA-allotted amount of low-quality elements that you all agree can make their way into the final experience.

The other thing to keep in mind here is the quote by film director Howard Hawks, in which he states a good movie is 'three great scenes and no bad ones.'[4] By focusing on consistency, even with lower peaks, it can create a scenario where there are 'no bad ones' and allow you to identify the key moments or features to apply extra attention so they can be truly great.

Fidelity and Density

Another approach to communicating quality is by separating the fidelity of individual animations from the density of animations required. Or, in other terms, quality and quantity. As an example, on the *Dragon Age* team, letter grades were assigned to quality targets, as opposed to numbers like 1–10. This was defined as follows:

- *A + Industry Leader*

- *A Above Industry Standards*

- *B At Industry Standards*

- *C Below Industry Standards*

With these, you can then assign released titles to each target grade to align expectations across the team. But like style, quality can mean different things. This is where breaking out quality between fidelity and density can help. For fidelity, the intent is to focus people's attention on the quality of the animation itself in terms of the fundamentals of animation. Density is focused on how much animation is required and available at any moment, including for the player, npcs and the world itself. The examples we used to define each target were as follows:

Target Comps in Terms of Animation Fidelity

- *A + Last of Us Part 2, Spider-Man: Miles Morales*

- *A God of War, Red Dead Redemption 2*

- *B Ghost of Tsushima, Jedi: Fallen Order, AC: Valhalla*

- *C Elden Ring, Mass Effect: Andromeda, Dragon Age: Inquisition*

Target Comps in Terms of Content Density

- *A Last of Us 2, Spider-Man, God of War*

- *B Jedi: Fallen Order, Final Fantasy 7*

- *C Mass Effect: Andromeda*

By separating the two, there is an allowance for flexibility in the quality and scope of the conversation. Consistency can then come from agreeing on a static grade in either Fidelity or Density and then allowing for variable grades in both, to define the peaks and valleys. I tend to agree on a consistent fidelity level while adjusting the density level to the priority of the feature. Which, if someone wants to create a competitive title in the AAA space, the definition of quality would be defined as follows:

B Fidelity Target + Variable Density Target = Overall Animation Quality Bar

Every team, project and relationship will likely require some variation of the above conversations and approaches to arrive at a quality bar. But something that will always be necessary are examples of what the highest and lowest acceptable quality look like, specifically for your project. This is where Completion Standards are valuable to define.

COMPLETION STANDARDS

This can go by different terms at different studios, but ultimately, what is being defined here is what stage of progress can be assigned to any piece of work. While clinical sounding compared to other terminology, there is a wonderful clarity to the term Completion Standards. It also allows you to customize the number of stages that best fit your team and project. For example, here is what Completion Standards (CS) enacted on *South of Midnight* mean at a high level.

- CS0
  - We Have a Plan

- CS1
  - Not Pretty but it Exists

- CS2
  - Conveys Craft Intent and Works Properly

- CS3
  - Ship It

- CS4

  - Hyper Polish

This structure can then be applied to every discipline and feature. But the specifics of what those entail for each discipline and feature need to be further clarified. In terms of animation, it is likely valuable to have clear definitions and examples across each group, like gameplay animation, technical animation, cinematics, etc. These are the valuable elements to define in terms of each CS stage.

- Discipline Expectations

- Requirements to Begin

- Quality & Commitment Level

- Required Approvers for Next Stage

- Feedback to Incorporate

- Examples

When applied to animation, this is how I like to define each of those elements. This chart should be easy to find as part of the wiki, as part of the production practices section discussed in the previous chapter. The information here should ideally be clear in what it is asking for. But it is worth discussing the intent behind each section after you read this over (Figure 9.2).

For *Expectations*, this is about establishing the goals and role of animation at each stage. It sets the tone in terms of priority, quality and needs of animation at each CS stage. It also allows for the time and space for animators to start thinking about the form and function required, with opportunities for both the conscious and unconscious minds to engage with the creative tasks at hand.

Requirements to Begin is to make sure a character, feature or scene is well enough understood to be ready for animation work to begin. Animation is all about communicating intent, and this section is specifically established to make sure the intent is clear enough to be communicated. And as a midstream discipline, this helps to make sure that, in terms of planning, production and dependencies, there is a clear understanding of how

Standard	Animation Expectations	Requirements to Begin	Quality & Commitment Level	Required Approvers for Next Stage	Feedback to Incorporate	Gameplay Example	Cinematic Example
CS0 *We Have a Plan*	**FEATURE DEFINITION** • Regularly COMMUNICATE with Feature Team • DEFINE a NEED for animation support	• Design Intent • Narrative Intent • Concept Sketches • Tech Investigations • Realization Intent	• Thumbnails • Reference Videos	• Feature Team (Primary) • Animation Leadership (Secondary)	• Required: Objective • Optional: Subjective	Ref Videos	Thumbnail Storyboards
CS1 *Not Pretty but it Exists*	**PLACEHOLDER WORK** • UNBLOCK team partners • VALIDATE and CLARIFY FUNCTION, CONTEXT and METRICS • Should try to convey intended animation vision, though not a priority	• Design Doc • Storyboard • Concept Art • Box/Proxy Model • 1st Pass Skinning/Rig	• Re-use • Quick Block Out • Rough Mocap • Temp System	• Feature Team (Primary) • Animation Leadership (Secondary)	• Required: Objective • Optional: Subjective	Block Out Animation	Animatic Layout
CS2 *Convey Craft Intent and Works Properly*	**ROUGH WORK** • REFINE and LOCK FUNCTION, CONTEXT and METRICS • Clearly communicates animation INTENT and VISION • POSING, TIMING and FEATURE LOCKED for downstream partners	• CS2 Approved Design • CS2 Approved VO • CS2 Approved Camera • CS2 Approved Art • CS2 Approved Rig/Skinning	• Timing & Intent Locked • Proper System	• Animation Leadership (Primary) • Feature Team (Secondary)	• Required: Objective • Optional: Subjective	1st Pass Animation	1st Pass Animation
CS3 *Ship It*	**SHIPPABLE WORK** • Animation STYLE and POLISH applied • Base QUALITY is achieved • Most animations considered complete on approval of this stage	• Locked Design • Locked VO • Locked Camera • Locked Art • Locked Rig/Skinning	• Standard Quality Bar • System Optimized	• Animation Leadership	• Optional: Objective	Completed Animation	Completed Animation
CS4 *Hyper Polish*	**HYPER POLISH** • Moments called out for additional attention and polish	• Requested by Leadership	• Gold Quality	• Animation Leadership	• Director Driven: Objective		

FIGURE 9.2   A chart that breaks down the specific details for each CS stage in terms of animation.

everything needs to fit together in the pipeline. This way, if someone from project leadership or production asks what it will take for an animation to be at any specific CS stage, you can point them to this chart.

The *Quality and Commitment Level* section is really an extension of the expectations, but with specific clarity as to what the creation methods and quality of output of the animation should be expected. This is as much for the animation team to understand how far to take their work for each stage as it is for other disciplines to understand the quality of work they will receive at each stage. Keeping animations at these stages allows for a balance between iteration, exploration and eventually polish, with minimal time and work lost to changes. It will also help to keep the animation team honest and accountable to downstream partners like vfx and audio.

Required for Approvers for Next Stage is important to call out, as it establishes the collaborative relationship inherent in the animation process. In the early CS stages, the purpose is to quickly iterate and prove out the functional needs of an action, feature or scene. But as the process moves on and the function is established and approved, execution on the form becomes the priority. By establishing the primary and secondary approvers at each stage, this should give the proper amount of insight and voice to everyone who needs it. We will get more into the approval process, as well as the intent behind calling out Objective and Subjective feedback, in the next chapter.

And finally, what all of this has been building up toward are the specific examples of what each stage looks like. In the above chart, I've included what those are likely to be for your project. But the key here is to include examples from your project. This takes all of the work around the vision and the completion standards and shows in very specific terms what the iteration and production process look like at every stage of the process. The best approach is to use examples of a single animation or scene. So make sure you save examples of the first creations to go through these steps. This allows you to attach the proving out of the production process to proving out a quality bar target animation or scene, which can help you get the cross-disciplinary support likely needed. The dream of every project is to have a quality bar target for one of every type of animation element by the time you leave pre-production, so that you can move into production with the confidence that all of your systems, tools and pipeline are in place to execute at shippable quality for the entire game.

Gold, Silver and Bronze

The use of Gold, Silver and Bronze as classification stages of work seems to be most often used for cinematics or narrative scenes. Though I have also seen it used in other areas and disciplines. The idea behind it is that there are three buckets that work can be placed into. Gold is meant to be the highest quality work and the intended highlight of the experience. Silver is then a step down, in that it should require some additional attention to make sure it meets slightly higher expectations than normal. And finally, Bronze, which is meant to be work that functionally meets expectations. The intent behind these is clear enough, but very quickly, this delineation can inform the creation process for each. We will use cinematics to show how this can happen and where the flaws in the approach present themselves.

Gold generally means custom-created cinematics with a more traditional film approach. This allows for animation to deliver on most anything written with the least number of creative and technical constraints required of the scene. Silver and Bronze then become some manner of machinima, creating scenes using a library of existing animations. The amount of time afforded to scenes is often the defining difference between a Silver and Bronze scene, though there is generally some amount of budget afforded to creating some custom animations to support Silver scenes requiring something that doesn't already exist in the animation library.

The problems with this approach come, when further into production, scenes need to be downgraded to meet scope, time or budget constraints. Scenes that were Gold get moved to Silver, and Silver then get moved to Bronze. While this might make sense at first blush, what has happened is that Gold, Silver and Bronze have come to represent not only quality but also the complexity of what is required by scenes. Gold was established to allow for any sort of performance between characters and likely require actions that the existing animation library doesn't support. Likewise, the Silver scenes were established to allow for some additional complexity of actions that will no longer be afforded if moved to Bronze.

This all means that if a scene is downgraded, it needs to be rewritten to match the constraints of the new scene type. But by the time these changes are made for scope reasons, scripts are often locked, VO might already have been recorded, and the ability to create custom animations isn't a guarantee. Which then means either consistency of quality is going to dip and/or a significant hidden crunch is being added to the project as animators and cinematic designers try to meet the demands of the scene with the limited resources at their disposal.

This all leads me to specifically deter teams from using the terms Gold, Silver and Bronze. As discussed at the start of this chapter, Complexity and Quality need to be defined separately, as the former defines the success of the latter. On the *Dragon Age* team, the approach was to remove not only the Gold, Silver and Bronze terms for cinematic scenes but also the idea of three tiers in general. Talking with the team, Silver was where the most scope creep, bugs and dips in the consistency of quality happened on past projects. This led to the delineation of either Custom scenes or Systemic scenes. The intent was that Custom scenes would function the way Gold always had, allowing for the realization of the most complex of scenes in terms of physicality and emotion. Systemic scenes were then designed to deliver the best Bronze scenes possible, with as much reactivity and flexibility as possible and as little friction as possible. This established clear constraints around what Systemic could conceivably achieve very early on, to help define the scope of scenes early on. Which then in turn cemented what the impact would be of changing a scene from Custom to Systemic later in development. If a scene was written that was beyond the constraints of what Systemic could achieve, then either the scene needed to be added to the Custom scene budget or it needed to be adjusted to meet the constraints of Systemic. This allows the tech and team to focus on creating the best versions of those two workflows and how well they can work together.

Ultimately, this becomes the perfect example of how clarifying Complexity can highlight issues in established workflows, which in turn lets you focus on building better approaches towards establishing a more consistent level of Quality across the experience.

NOTES

1 Reading Amanda Montell's book *Cultish: The Language of Fantaticism* (2021) will very quickly change how you perceive the way people communicate as well as the cultures of studios that embrace different levels of cult-like language. For both better and worse.

2 Paired with the above book, Barbara Ehrenreich's *Bright-sided: How Positive Thinking is Undermining America* (2010) will almost certainly change how you approach communication. The history of relentless positivity across business, religion and health is one everyone in a leadership position would

do well to study and understand. Byung-Chul Han's *The Burnout Society* (2015) also looks at constant positivity from a philosophical angle, and how that contributes to burnout, among other personal and cultural issues.

3 While I am again referencing Nicholas Sammond's *Birth of an Industry: Blackface Minstrelsy and the Rise of American Animation* (2015) in terms of the history of production and who it chooses to celebrate, the core point of the book is one we should all be aware of in this industry.

4 The quote *'three great scenes and no bad ones'* seems to be a paraphrase of an answer Howard Hawks repeated throughout his career, first as part of a discussion at the 1970 Chicago Film Festival, eventually transcribed and published by Joseph McBride in *Focus on Howard Hawks* (1972). The number of great scenes seems to vary between two and five, as well as whether they should be good or great. But what remains clear throughout the various versions of the quote is that there should be no bad or annoying scenes. Which sits at the heart of consistency being the foundation of quality.

CHAPTER 10

Defining Scope

THE STRUCTURE, APPROACH AND focus of production processes will very much influence the success of the animation vision in the game. Even when you have made the effort to define a vision that communicates the intent of the project, if you are not mindful of the production needs of the project, the vision will almost certainly suffer. But like anything, balance is the key, as too much production structure or process will weigh down a team and the creative vision. This means you want to always have a solid understanding of the scope and dependencies of the work required to deliver on the experience of the project.

As discussed in Chapter 3, there is an inherent tension between the creative process and production requirements. But that tension can be a powerful tool to drive decision-making and problem-solving. It is when production and creatives are not speaking in a shared language that the tension can boil over, causing problems. The solution is then how best to translate between the languages of creation and production.

Something to keep in mind with all of this is how much the project structure will influence the amount of time and effort you will need to spend translating between creation and production. If the project and studio structure are set up to have producers at the top, with directors answering to production, then a fair amount of a director's time will be spent translating creative needs into the language of production. If producers answer to directors, then likely the inverse is true, with producers translating production needs into the language of creatives. Like anything, there are pros and cons to both approaches, and how successful

 DOI: 10.1201/9781003356196-10

they are largely depends on how strong the communication and trust are between the two groups. Which means in either case, you want to make sure you are conscious of production needs and how to speak the language to strengthen both communication and trust.[1]

HIGH-LEVEL COST SHEET

As early as possible, it can be incredibly valuable to start working on a high-level cost sheet. The goal here is to create a checkpoint against the initial team size estimates before you are able to fully scope out characters, features and scenes in more detail. This is likely something that can be done concurrently with defining the vision, as the two can inform one another. What you are looking for here is:

- The player character needs
- The non-playable character needs
- The different types of non-playable characters
- The estimated number of minutes of narrative scenes
- The different types of narrative scenes
- The competitive targets
- Previous project scope

With these, you can create a rough, high-level sheet, to get a sense of the overall scope of the project. To illustrate an example, here is a template sheet[2] for a fictional 3rd-person, narrative-driven, action-adventure game with a constant over-the-shoulder camera. While this isn't directly from any specific game I have worked on, it should give you a sense of the level of estimation and the type of information you want to convey (Figure 10.1). Everything here should be best guesses, but informed by some consistent logic and past experiences. For gameplay, think of everything in terms of small, medium and large amounts of time. Then assign a set number of weeks to each side. For this example, small is 5 weeks, medium is 10 and large is 20. But there are several variables to consider when setting these values. Namely, complexity, quality and effort. What is the complexity and quality of the feature? How much friction is in the workflow? How experienced is the team in making this feature? How much new tech is required

GAMEPLAY

	Player Character	Friendly NPC	Enemy NPC	World NPC
Locomotion		Weeks to Create		
On Ground	20	10	10	5
In Air	10	0	5	0
Extended	5	5	5	0
Narrative	5	5	5	0
Combat		Weeks to Create		
Core Attacks	20	10	10	0
Abilities	10	10	0	0
Ultimates	5	0	0	0
Takedowns	20	0	0	0
Hit Reactions	5	10	10	0
Death	5	5	5	0
Interactions		Weeks to Create		
Pickup	5	0	0	0
Open Door	5	0	0	0
Pull Lever	5	0	0	0
Character Types		Weeks to Create		
Number of Characters	2	4	7	15
Total Weeks to Create	240	240	350	75

NARRATIVE

	Cinematics	Scripted Events
Custom	Minutes in Game	
	120	0
Systemic	Minutes in Game	
	240	0
Complex	Minutes in Game	
	0	60
Simple	Minutes in Game	
	0	120
Total Minutes in Game	360	180
Weeks to Create each Minute	2	3
Total Weeks to Create	720	540

TOTAL WEEKS

Gameplay	905
Narrative	1260
Last Project	
Gameplay	750
Narrative	1200
Difference	
Gameplay	155
Narrative	60

# of Team Members

Current	
Gameplay	8
Narrative	10
Required	
Gameplay	21
Narrative	28
Difference	
Gameplay	13
Narrative	18

CAPTURE COSTS

	Shoot Days (Weeks/Day)
Player (30/day)	8
Friendly NPC (30/day)	8
Enemy NPC (40/day)	9
World NPC (30/day)	3
Custom Cinematics (30/day)	8
Systemic Cinematics (60/day)	8
Scripted Events (40/day)	14
Cost/Shoot Day	
Mocap	$20,000.00
Pcap	$40,000.00
Totals	
Mocap Shoot Days	50
Pcap Shoot Days	8
Mocap Cost	$1,000,000.00
Pcap Cost	$320,000.00
Last Project	
Shoot Days	30
Mocap Cost	$650,000.00
Pcap Cost	$150,000.00
Difference	
Shoot Days	20
Mocap Cost	$350,000.00
Pcap Cost	$170,000.00

FIGURE 10.1 A sheet that breaks down the high-level scope and cost of the project.

to pull it off? I would classify the 5, 10 and 20 estimates towards the higher end of complexity, quality and effort. A less experienced team with a less robust workflow on a game with average quality and effort could also require these sorts of estimates. But when in doubt, round up and expect things to take more time. We all naturally tend to underestimate how long anything will take to finish, so if you feel like you are overestimating you are most likely closer to the actual target.

As a rule of thumb, for sheets with lots of numbers, it is worthwhile denoting cells that have manually entered information and cells that are being generated by formulas. In the above example, the shaded cells with numbers are being generated by formulas, and the unshaded cells are what require manual input.

For narrative content, it tends to be that early on there is a goal of how many minutes of narrative scenes the team is aiming for. This is fine, as you can use past experiences and workflows to estimate how many weeks it took in the past to create one minute of narrative content. With that, you can get weeks to create estimates, similar to gameplay.

From here, you can get a sense of how many weeks of work are going to be required on the project and how many team members will be required to create the work. After tallying the total weeks of work required, you can find the number of team members required by dividing the total weeks by 45, which is the average number of work weeks in North America. However, this can vary by country and company, so it is worth checking how your studio and project estimate the average number of work weeks in a year.

Next, if your project plans on partnering with an external capture stage, then this is a perfect time to start getting some estimates in terms of the capture days needed and the budget required to capture. This is by far the most gut-driven estimate on the sheet, as translating weeks of work to specific capture needs does not have a 1:1. There are variables like how much of the animation is keyframe vs capture, optical vs inertial, reuse of captured data across characters, etc. So for this, I used weeks of work that could be captured in a day. I used 30 as a base set, as that gave a general number for the player that matched what my gut expectations were. And in general, player animation is the area I have had the most experience with and feel most confident with my gut. From there, I adjusted the days of each area based on whether they tend to be able to capture more or less data in a day than a player animation suite. Maybe you are more experienced in one of the other areas and would prefer to use that as a starting point. For example, if you know with relative certainty how many weeks it takes to create a minute of cinematic data and how many minutes of cinematic data you can capture in a shoot day, then that can be a fantastic ground truth to inform your estimates. Again, the point here isn't to get it perfect, as that will come from more in-depth tracking sheets. What you are looking for here is to be in the ballpark, to check against the initial guesses from the team size calculator.

The last bits are to include the cost of capture per day and totals from the last project. All in an effort to understand and display as early as possible the delta between current resources and the proposed scope of the project. Almost every game I have worked on has seen the scope to be well over current resources and beyond the last project, to a similar percentage as what this example sheet displays. This isn't meant to panic anyone, but to inform project leadership of where the current trajectory is headed. And the areas and opportunities most in need of support.

Obviously, scope cuts can make a big difference here, as changing any of the multipliers, like the number of characters, can quickly show the impact that would have in terms of the number of team members and capture costs required. It can spark conversations around why certain estimates are higher, such as scripted events taking more time to create than cinematics. Which may come down to workflow issues that, when addressed, can make for faster creation times. It can also demonstrate the value of investing in an internal capture solution, as the cost of setting up a stage and hiring a team to run it may be lower and allow for more flexibility.

Often, in pre-production, people are encouraged to have their heads in the clouds and think big. Which is fine enough at the beginning of pre-production. But by the end of pre-production, the team needs to have landed on the ground and be moving towards the goal. Having a sheet like this around 1/3 of the way through pre-production can help keep the blue-sky ideas from turning into pie-in-the-sky ideas. And give people a chance to recognize the sky from the ground, to allow for the landing to happen as smoothly as possible.

SCOPE TRACKING SHEETS

If the goal of pre-production is to understand everything needed for each element of the game, towards the end of pre-production, you should be able to create individual tracking sheets for each character in the project.[3] Being able to break down the needs for each character can then allow you to create more solid estimates to further validate or contradict the high-level tracking sheet made earlier in pre-production (Figure 10.2).

Every project has different production processes and tools to track scope. These sheets are not meant to be used instead of those production processes, but to inform them. Often, project tracking software or project-wide sheets are not well suited for the granularity required for every animation needed for a character. That is where these sheets are valuable. The trick will be how to integrate these into that pipeline, but let's first look at what these sheets can look like. Every project likely requires some variations on what the most important information is for these sheets. But there are some specific elements here that should absolutely be core to any you use.

To start, it is a good idea to think of the different groups or systems of animation required for a character. In the case of this sheet, those are:

- Explore in Place

- Explore Traversal

- Extended Traversal

- Combat in Place

- Combat Traversal

- Hit Reactions

- Combat Attacks

- Abilities

By creating these groups, you can then break down all of the animations required to realize each. This also allows you to quickly visualize and track the work required for each group at a higher level. This is important, as this is likely the level of information that most naturally fits into the larger tracking software or sheets of the project. In this case, the *Phase Gate* and *Combined Estimates* are the important elements to track by group. By having this bucket track all updates to the individual animations within, it will then allow anyone using this sheet to quickly inform and update any other tracking resource. Which is to say, double check that these are the groups that also best fit the project's tracking needs.

Animation Groups	Phase Gate	Priority	Notes	Animate	Implement	Combined	OS	Rig Status
- REFERENCE -	Completed							Proxy
- EXPLORE IN PLACE -	CS1: In Progress		7.6					
- EXPLORE TRAVERSAL -	CS1: In Progress		96					
- EXTENDED TRAVERSAL -	CS1: In Progress		29					
Jump In Place	Not Started	P1	Are metrics for this locked?	3	1	4	No	
Jump Moving	CS1: In Progress	P1		2	1	3	No	
Fall Loop	CS1: In Progress	P1		1	1	2	No	
Jump Land In Place	CS1: In Progress	P1		1	1	2	No	
Jump Land Moving	CS1: In Progress	P2	Need to dial in if we need per locomotion speed. Can we repurpose starts?	1	1	3	No	
Double Jump	CS1: In Progress	P1		3	1	4	No	
Long Fall Loop	CS1: In Progress	P2		2	1	3	No	
Long Fall Soft Land	CS1: In Progress	P2		2	1	3	No	
Mantle From Ground	CS1: In Progress	P1	How many variants? Directionality?	2	1	3	No	
Mantle From Air	Not Started	P1		1	1	2	No	
- COMBAT IN PLACE -	CS1: In Progress		17.1					
- COMBAT TRAVERSAL -	CS1: In Progress		14.25					
- HIT REACTIONS -	CS1: In Progress		10.75					
- COMBAT ATTACKS -	CS1: In Progress		40					
- ABILITIES -	CS1: In Progress		36					

Phase	Animate	Implement	Combined	OS	P1	P2	P3
Not Started	96.5	33.5	130	5	81.25	36	12.25
CS1: In Progress	68	31.2	99.2	19.25	82.7	9	0
CS2: In Progress	3	0.5	3.5	0	3.5	0	0
CS3: In Progress	16	2	18	0	18	0	0
CS4: In Progress	0	0	0	0	0	0	0
Completed							
Total Days Remaining	183.5	67.2	250.7	24.25	185.45	45	12.25

OS Ready Files: 11

OS Complete Files: 0

FIGURE 10.2 A sheet that breaks down the individual scope and cost for a single character.

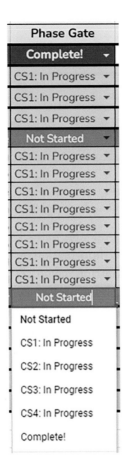

FIGURE 10.3   A segment of the tracking sheet that shows the completion standard options available for any animation.

Once you have established groups and have listed all the animations required for each group, it is valuable to track the level of completion. In this example, you can see the option to choose what completion standard the current animation is at. I also like to color code the entire row by the state of completion so that you can get a quick, high-level view of how far along a character is simply by looking at the sheet (Figure 10.3).

The next column on the sheet is *Priority*, which is especially useful when first establishing these sheets. This allows you to start these sheets with as many animations as you may think is possible, but forces you to assign a priority that allows for conversations around if it is needed or desired. This also works well to clarify which animations need to be worked on first to prove the core of a character.

Animate	Implement	Combined	OS
1	0.1	1.1	No ▾
5	1	6	No ▾
5	0.5	5.5	Ready ▾

FIGURE 10.4 A segment of the tracking sheet that shows the different columns used to estimate the time required to complete an animation.

Having a *Notes* section is valuable to track questions or notes that come up in reviews, list out metric information or include animation ideas presented by other disciplines during the process of development.

The next columns are all about estimating the time required to complete each animation. What is important to point out here is that instead of a single estimate, it is better to split the estimate into two categories. The amount of time required to create the animation itself. And the amount of time required to implement the animation into the game (Figure 10.4).

Breaking up estimates in this way is valuable for several reasons. The first is that it gets estimates to think more holistically about the work required to consider an animation complete. It allows you to highlight and track how much time is required to implement animation into the game and recognize areas or systems that would benefit from workflows with less complexity or friction. This is also beneficial when considering outsource support, as often the implementation work is still required by the internal term.

Which leads to the *Outsource* (OS) column. This column allows for animations to be flagged as ready for outsourcing, which, beyond the immediate value of knowing what is available for external partners, allows you to then automatically adjust internal time estimates based on what is being sent out. All of which culminates in the *Total Estimates* section of the sheet (Figure 10.5).

Here you can see the totals of everything being tracked by phase, priority and outsource support. The animate estimates are adjusted to take into account work that is outsourced, while maintaining the implement estimates to remain internal. At which point, you can now visualize this in any number of ways, as well as link to it in any number of other places. Generally, I also like to create another high-level sheet that displays the

	Animate	Implement	Combined	OS	P1	P2	P3
Not Started	96.5	33.5	130	5	81.25	36	12.25
CS1: In Progress	68	31.2	99.2	19.25	82.7	9	0
CS2: In Progress	3	0.5	3.5	0	3.5	0	0
CS3: In Progress	16	2	18	0	18	0	0
CS4: In Progress	0	0	0	0	0	0	0
Complete!							
Total Days Remaining	183.5	67.2	250.7	24.25	185.45	45	12.25
				OS Ready Files			
				11			
				OS Complete Files			
				0			

FIGURE 10.5   A segment of the tracking sheet that shows the totals of everything being tracked in the sheet.

level of completion and time remaining for each character. It is also valuable to track the status of the rig at both this and the high level, as a way to make sure the CS level of the animation is in line with the appropriate CS level of the rig.

As an example of high-level tracking sheets as art, here is one created by Jeremy Yates, while he was Lead Animator on Uncharted 3. Seeing this is what awoke in me a desire and appreciation for what we should all aspire towards understanding with these sorts of sheets (Figure 10.6).

With these tracking sheets, you can be production-ready, able to move forward with confidence on what it will take to complete every character in the game, generate future shot lists for capture and coordinate dependencies with upstream partners.

UPSTREAM DEPENDENCIES

Gathering and sorting all this information will quickly fall flat if it isn't properly integrated into the larger production process. There is no purpose in building a beautiful set of gears if they aren't hooked into the larger machine. This is also something you should expect to be proactive about as someone in a midstream discipline leadership role. Often times, projects track the high-level feature estimate, most likely aligned with and driven by disciplines upstream of animation. And afford disciplines downstream from animation separate, staggered deadlines. Which can often squeeze midstream disciplines, like animation. This means that unless you have a

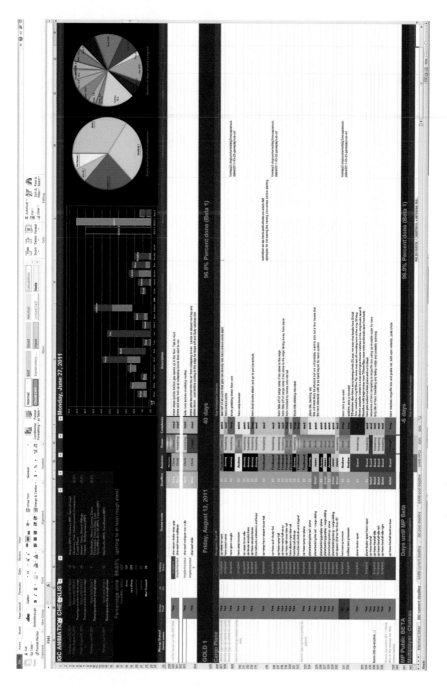

FIGURE 10.6   An animation tracking sheet created by Jeremy Yates for *Uncharted 3*.

dedicated animation producer to help coordinate and communicate these dependencies, this is something you will want to consciously plan for and regularly communicate to project leadership and production partners.

Upstream Questions

One part of being proactive is to build upon the design needs discussed in Chapter 2, in terms of clarifying the functional needs separate from the form requests. This is really an extension of the definition of acting.

'Acting is ACTION in Pursuit of an OBJECTIVE, Trying to Overcome an OBSTACLE.'

What animation is looking for from upstream teams is an objective and an obstacle. Those are the functions. The action is then the form in response to the function. When upstream requests come in only the form of an action, that is when a consistent and cohesive character performance is most likely to be lost.

The more collaborative teams are, the more this following approach will become natural to how each discipline thinks and works alongside one another. But regardless of a collaborative partnership or a service provider relationship, it can be helpful to have some standard questions to establish within tracking sheets or as part of task request descriptions to make sure the function is being defined. I've also included examples of the sort of answers and information you should expect and be looking for with these questions.

- *What is the design function and metrics?*

  - *gap closer*

    - *3 m horizontal, 1m vertical gap closer*

  - *single target attack*

    - *0.3 second hit, 0.6 second early exit, causes light hit reaction on target*

  - *interact with collectable object*

    - *45° forward-facing angle required to activate*

    - *up to 3 m away from object*

    - *player controlled camera*

- *What is the narrative function?*

  - *emotional reaction to new information*

  - *completion of goal*

  - *awareness of a new objective*

  - *strengthen a relationship between characters*

- *What is the tone?*

  - *serious and dramatic*

  - *general use for any tone*

  - *light-hearted and fun*

- *What happens before and after this?*

  - *can happen on ground or in the air*

  - *happens at the end of a combo chain*

  - *scene is triggered by squeeze through crack animation and ends in combat*

- *Does this need variants or progression?*

  - *contextual versions needed for exploration and combat states*

  - *can unlock the ability to charge the attack*

    - *charged attack 6 second hit, 1.5 second to early exit, knocks target to ground*

- *Do you have a suggestion for the form?*

  - *front flip to cross the gap*

  - *horizontal slash like Dark Souls 1 handed sword light attack*

  - *generic fiddle interaction to open chests or pick flowers*

  - *character is smug like Han Solo*

All of these are the sorts of questions upstream partners should be able to answer without too much issue if there is a clear understanding of the need and purpose of the feature, scene or action. If an upstream partner is unable to answer these questions, then it is a good indication that the animation support should be rough, block out versions to help quickly prototype and find the intent of what is required.

It can be valuable to have these questions required as part of the feature tracking list or request forms, as it helps to ingrain the specifics of what animation needs to be able to communicate both the design and narrative function in a way that fits with the overall intent of the character's performance. It is to that last point that it is important to ask for suggestions on the action or performance, as the upstream partner might have something very specific in mind that may or may not fit with the overall performance, as defined in Chapter 6. Adding it as a suggestion gives a space for the conversation to be had as to why it may or may not fit. And possibly inform some additional information expected from the function or needs that were not called out otherwise. But it very much helps to expand the conversation of actions and performance beyond what looks 'cool' or was most recently seen within popular media.

Workflow Charts

With the complexity of interdependencies across multiple disciplines, charting out the complete workflow can be an incredibly valuable way of illustrating the process for everyone to see and understand. Especially for teams working together for the first time or on projects that have more complexity than in the past, this can be a great way of mapping out dependencies and expectations of involvement across all the required disciplines.

These can be as in-depth or high-level as your specific team and project require. The longer a team has worked together or their familiarity with the complexity required for the type of project, the less detail is likely to be required (Figure 10.7).

In a lot of ways, this is a visualization of the completion standards discussed in the previous chapter and lays the groundwork for the review and approval process discussed in more detail in the next chapter. But it is valuable to create this as a communication tool for upstream and production partners as well as the animation team itself. With this in mind, the key points to include here are:

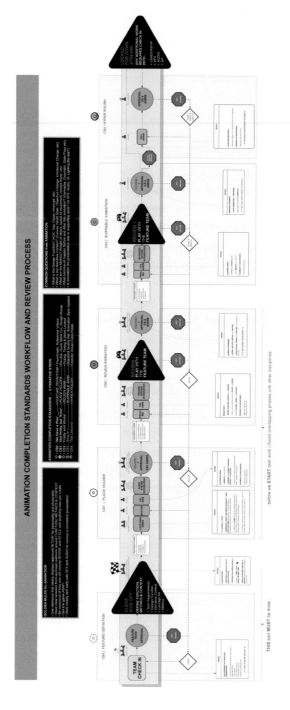

FIGURE 10.7   The workflow chart for animation at Compulsion Games.

- *Dependencies and Requirements to Begin*

- *Disciplines Responsible for Each Step*

- *Cross-Disciplinary Review Points*

- *Required Approvers*

It can be valuable to add break-out details to any section, such as what specific terminology is being used at specific steps or the approval requirements at each review. This can also be a valuable place to add key information related to other disciplines, such as the upstream questions presented above.

Once established, you should all create something following this exact process to prove it out. You may find there were specific steps you missed. You may find yourself overcomplicating several steps. But as valuable as mapping out the process can be, working through it proves that the team actually understands the process. This is the universal truth of game development. No matter how great a plan looks, until you put it into action, you are making the best guesses.

After creating and then validating the workflow chart, the continued value of it and how much it will be used are honestly variable. It certainly starts with you engaging and creating it in good faith, with a focus on conveying the right amount of information that matches the trust and understanding of each person involved in the process. Too much information will push people away. The example I showed above comes dangerously close to doing just that. In fact, for some more senior teams that have worked together for a while, it is almost certainly too much.

Beyond the amount of information being conveyed, the visual design will also play an important part in how much people want to engage with the graph. Graphic design is not a personal strong suite of mine, so like with the slide decks, I look to start using something already created by someone on the team with a better sense of design. Chances are someone on the UI or production teams already has something that you can use as a foundation to get you well on your way to a better-looking design.

The final step towards people using this comes down to how often you use and refer to it during reviews, kick-offs and questions of dependencies and priorities. Which is honestly true of all of the vision, production and reference communication devices you create. It does not matter how much time and effort you put into making anything if you then hide it away to never look at it again. If that is how you engage with all of these things, you can expect the rest of the team to do the same. In the specific case of these workflow charts, the exercise of creating and working through them may have been enough for teams to understand the process.

Production Roadmaps and Deadlines

Everything in this chapter has been building towards the ultimate production goal of being able to project a deadline for when the project can be completed. Team velocity trackers, burndown charts, Gantt charts and time line graphs are all various realizations of a roadmap meant to plot a course towards a finish line. While there are always external variables beyond the estimates and dependencies defined by the teams, such as project budgets, optimal release windows and unexpected obstacles, the hope is always that the deadline aligns with the estimates and dependency requirements defined by the team. And if they don't align, there is always the option to delay the release.

As Shigeru Miyamoto is often quoted, *'A delayed game is eventually good, but a rushed game is forever bad.'* However, not every project is given the option to push its deadlines. And in some cases, pushing a deadline can cause as many issues as it solves. So instead of showing various visualizations of roadmaps or projected deadlines, what is important here are some points to keep in mind when discussing how these are created, presented and the best approaches when the projected timeline doesn't match the business-required timeline.

When the roadmaps are first being created or discussed, you should ask how they are handling staggered deadlines by each discipline. Trying to include that on a high-level roadmap can quickly turn into a bunch of noise. But ideally, that can point to a roadmap at a feature or mechanic level that takes the workflow chart into account and has staggered deadlines to match the dependencies required to finish any task. This is a better approach than having different deadlines for each discipline presented on a high-level roadmap, as it shows how work across disciplines can happen simultaneously across different features, mechanics or characters. And if the team size allows it, the tasks for each person in the group so that you can see what everyone is working on in relation to one another and when they are expecting to finish their work. This can all become very complex very quickly if you have more than a couple of people on your team, so the value of a production partner who can do all of this well is worth their weight in gold. With everything created up to this point, they should be able to weave a beautiful tapestry of production deadlines and dependency charts.

The next important element to understand about a roadmap is the expectations of each phase and deadline. Alpha, beta, content complete, content lock, polish, bug fixing and post-production can all have different definitions and meanings at different studios on different projects. What you are ultimately looking for in any of these terms and timelines is when the blast door is going to start closing in terms of the team being able to check in updated or polished work. And when the blast door will close entirely, short of project leadership-approved changes.

If it isn't called out in the roadmap, ask about the team roll-off plans. Ideally, there is another project for the team to move onto after the current one wraps, and they are likely expecting team members to join and help prove out their project needs. Do not assume you will have every team member at the peak of production all the way until the end. Even losing one or two people can impact a schedule by weeks. In the same way, make sure holidays and time off are taken into account. Holidays are straightforward to include, but time off may be accounted for in different ways. Maybe there was a buffer in each estimate to take into account the overall percentage of time off, like with the estimates in the tracking sheet above. Maybe the project is adding an overall buffer of time off to the schedule as a whole to take into account PTO, sick days and other unforeseen changes to people's schedules. All of these are unknowns to a certain degree, so more than the details themselves, the bigger takeaway here is to understand how much of this has been included in the deadlines at all.

Which leads to polishing or post-production time. More and more projects are adding dedicated time to specifically polish them. Beyond what the expectations and definitions of that mean, it is important to understand when there will be external feedback review sessions held during that phase and how much of a response is expected to happen at that time. This will be covered in more detail in the next chapter on how to respond to external feedback and iteration. But the biggest takeaway here is to knowingly prioritize what you and the team want to accomplish during that time. As the blast door closes, it will be harder and harder to update and polish the work you all individually value. So spending some time up front to understand the places to polish with the most impact, be it for external reception or internal morale building, is worth planning.

All of this is to say that in many ways, animation is often the point where many strings of the project become braided together for other disciplines on the project. Being that midstream connection point means that it is important to understand the needs of upstream and tie them together in a way that allows those downstream from animation to have a clear and concise path forward with their work. The more care and appreciation you pay towards clarifying the scope and production processes within the animation team, the more it will be felt and appreciated by your vfx and audio peers.

NOTES

1 The Rosetta Stone of translating the languages of Production and Art is Rob Austin and Lee Devin's *Arftul Making: What Managers Need to Know About How Artists Work* (2003). It looks at the overlap in process between agile development methods and theater rehearsals and contains such nuggets of wisdom as 'Like it or not, artists have something useful to say to business people. Let's get used to that.'and 'We do this to consider the activities of artists in their own terms... it was our experience during this project that we missed the points artists were trying to make when we insisted on translating their ideas into management concepts already familiar and comfortable to us.' As far as I am concerned, this book is required reading for anyone in a leadership or production role. It was recommended to me just as I was locking down the writing of this book and I realize that a lot of what I discuss here in terms of communicating production and process is a variation of what they expertly covered there.

2 You can find the referenced sample document as part of the supplemental package on the book's website. The document is titled Scope Docs, and it is the HighLevel tab specifically being referenced here.

3 You can find the referenced sample document as part of the supplemental package on the book's website. The document is titled Scope Docs, and it is the CharacterTrackSheet tab specifically being referenced here.

CHAPTER 11

Reviews, Approvals and Feedback

THE VISION IS IN place. The scope is understood. What remains is execution of the plan. This transitions the role of the team from defining the shape and size of the box to now filling the box as full as possible. In an ideal world, this would align with when the project is transitioning into full production. However, when a project, team or feature is fully out of pre-production and into full production isn't always so clear to define. Sometimes it feels like it is happening in slow motion, and other times it can feel forced to happen suddenly. A lot of what has been covered up to this point has had the dual purpose of not only defining a clear vision but also a resilient one, able to adapt to any production schedule. However, the last step of that resilience is the ability to prove the vision in action, at scale. Which is where a clear review, approval and feedback process becomes key.

DEFINE THE REVIEW PROCESS

Reviews are something everyone within an animation team should be familiar with. Though some people respond to reviews and feedback differently than others, some actively focus on what can be improved, some on what they think might be an interesting alternative and others on only the positive. People also have different natural strengths, with some being stronger in terms of technique and some in creativity. They also tend to

DOI: 10.1201/9781003356196-11

naturally lean towards one part of the production process over another, such as prototyping over polishing. The longer you have worked with someone, the more these attributes become apparent. For newer team members, this is something you should be thinking about when talking to them about expectations from Chapter 1. And on top of all of this, how people deliver feedback in reviews can vary based on how they were trained, their personalities and their cultural backgrounds.

With all these variables amongst the team, defining a clear review process becomes all the more necessary as a consistent point everyone can return to. The other point of consistency in the review process is your own personal style of review. Which is to say, the approach to reviews should fit not only your own sensibilities but those that best suit the team's. There are specific elements of a review process you will want to adjust to best match the team and project.

Structure

Reviews often come in both formal and informal methods. Formal methods are along the lines of dailies or approval meetings, where there is a specific structure for defining a time, place and purpose for the review. Informal reviews are less structured feedback methods, like walk-throughs, impromptu requests to look at something or more casual show-and-tell sessions. While the inherent structure of each is what separates the two, it is valuable to be intentional about how both are used on the team. The value of an intentional structure for formal reviews is more readily apparent as the team gets into full production and needs to deliver on quality targets. But even for the informal reviews, you want to set up some general guidelines or best practices around how and where that feedback should be expected. Especially for teams that are hybrid or entirely remote, it can be easy to have informal reviews lead to mixed feedback. The following elements are what you want to keep in mind for both forms of reviews.

Cadence

How often should both the informal and formal review processes happen is a good place to start. Does it make sense to have dailies for formal reviews? Or do weeklies better suit the work? Should there be an office-hours approach to soliciting informal feedback, or is there an anytime, open-door policy for informal reviews? Should the informal include dedicated mentorship time between more senior team members providing feedback to less senior members? The answers to these questions will depend on the needs of the project, the complexity of the work the team is doing, their general experience level and the specific work style of each team member.

For more complex work being done by more senior members, the time frame desired between both formal and informal is likely longer, so that they can focus on completing the tasks at hand with as few distractions as possible. For less complex work and fewer senior team members, having more regular reviews of each type is likely necessary. If the work is complex and the person is less senior, it can be valuable to allow a full open door informal option with more regular formal reviews as opportunities to check in without smothering.

If you aren't intentional about the cadence of feedback and reviews, people will tend towards their own approaches, which can lead to chaos as some people only like to show work when they feel good about it. And others like to share or ask for feedback all the time, which can become a distraction to other team members. Establishing clarity of desired cadence for feedback then naturally leads to the next elements to consider.

Format and Location

How should people be showing their work and where should they be showing it? Should it be videos or builds of the game people should play to review? Does it need to be something where people gather together or can it happen asynchronously through different communication or review platforms? If it is in person, how is the feedback tracked? All of these again vary based on the team members themselves and if the team is in person, hybrid or remote. But like with cadence, if you are not intentional in defining guidelines, then people will default to their personal approaches, which can lead to inconsistent feedback and review experiences for each team member.

I personally value asynchronous review methods, as they allow people to define a time and place that work best for them when reviewing the work. But again, cadence needs to be taken into account here, with the person requesting the feedback defining a deadline they need feedback by. Does it need to be within the hour or the day? You don't want the asynchronous nature to slow down the feedback process or have things slip through the cracks, so assigning a deadline to the person needing to provide feedback can help them prioritize it accordingly. And if they don't, then the person asking for the feedback can assume there are no notes and continue on with their work.

Objective vs Subjective Feedback

Feedback generally falls into two categories. Objective and subjective. Objective feedback is focused on the fundamentals of the craft. Balance, physics, aesthetics and anything else that can be defined as objectively correct or incorrect. These notes are almost universally valuable and should be addressed to improve quality, unless stated otherwise by team leadership.

Subjective feedback can best be summed up as, 'You know what would be cool…' Changes in performance, type of movement or tone would all be subjective feedback. These sorts of notes can be better or different from what is being created, which is why it is important to separate them from objective feedback. By doing this, you can clarify a time and place for each type of feedback. Which is to say, as something has the intent and direction locked down with only polish remaining, the time for subjective feedback is largely over. By clarifying when objective and subjective feedback should be addressed as either required or optional, the team can feel confident in knowing what type of feedback they should be giving and responding to as their work moves throughout the completion standards process.

When you combine all of these elements together, you can start to map out a review process that best suits the team and project. As an example, this is the first pass review process we enacted at Compulsion (Figure 11.1).

Feedback Tone and Style

A lot of conversations around reviews can be focused on the tone or communication style that should be used when delivering feedback. But when it comes to the way feedback is conveyed, there is no one way or best way

Standard	Informal Review Expectations	Formal Review Format & Location	Approvers	Feedback to Incorporate
CS0 *We Have a Plan*	• In person, Slack or Syncsketch as defined by kickoff	• Video on Slack	• Feature Team • Animation Leadership	• Required: Objective • Optional: Subjective
CS1 *Not Pretty but it Exists*	• Required - In person, Slack or Syncsketch iteration with feature partners • Recommended- Slack or Syncsketch feedback from animation leadership	• In game video on Slack OR • Play in Gym	• Feature Team (Primary) • Animation Leadership (Secondary)	• Required: Objective • Optional: Subjective
CS2 *Conveys Craft Intent & Works Properly*	• Required - In person, Slack or Syncsketch iteration with feature partners • Required - Syncsketch feedback from animation leadership	• Play in Gym	• Animation Team Leadership (Primary) • Feature Team (Secondary)	• Required: Objective • Optional: Subjective
CS3 *Ship It*	• Required - Syncsketch feedback from approvers	• Play in game in Full Level	• Animation Team Leadership	• Optional: Objective
CS4 *Hyper Polish*	• Required - Syncsketch feedback from approvers	• Play in game in Full Level	• Animation Team Leadership	• Director Driven: Objective

FIGURE 11.1 An example of review and approval guidelines.

to communicate feedback. It will likely need to vary based on the level of trust, experience, personal sensibilities, studio culture, regional culture and overall ability of the team to communicate the vision. What is universal is the need for respect and good faith to be at the core of all feedback that is given and received. This is why unverisal feedback methods like the 'compliment sandwich' are at best cliché, and at worst, insulting. It is up to you to understand where the team is in terms of the way they give and receive feedback and make sure it aligns to meet the needs of the team. Simply forcing your feedback style onto the team or accepting a style that isn't aligned with the rest of the team is neither showing respect nor acting in good faith towards anyone. If the team is incredibly experienced and all business, conveying enthusiastic praise for everything big and small will cause them to be suspicious of your taste and ability to understand the complexities of the work. If it is a less experienced team or one that is still getting a sense of how they will all work together, a more hard-nosed approach that is light on praise is almost certainly going to have people put up walls. Likely, you will have people across this spectrum on your team, so it is important for you to adjust your approach to meet them where they are. Though it is also your responsibility to lead team members that are outliers in how they give and receive feedback back towards the rest of the team. The goal is to not force everyone to deliver feedback in the exact same way, with the same tone or style. The goal is for everyone to trust and respect their team members and follow your example of leaning in towards each other's feedback style. The closer the styles, the less they have to lean and the easier it becomes for each to trust the other without feeling like they are going to fall flat on their faces when they lean in. If you find the style and tone of feedback and communication on your team are still not connecting, there is a thriving industry of books available on the topic of leadership and feedback.[1]

Creating a clear feedback structure and culture will directly contribute to a stronger sense of trust and community within a team. Consistency in the review process and the way it is communicated will help the team share their work earlier, and trusting the feedback will be valuable. And that ability to give and receive constructive feedback shows a sense of respect for the person and the work, which then builds comradery amongst the team. The time you take to foster constructive feedback will lead to a much stronger foundation for the team as a whole.

DEFINE THE APPROVAL PROCESS

While the review and approval processes are largely linked, there are some additional elements to keep in mind when it comes to approvals. These are all things to keep in mind if you find you need additional structure applied to the approval process.

Completion Standard Examples

Before something can be approved, there need to be guidelines or requirements for it to pass or fail. These should be part of the completion standards process as defined in Chapter 9. But better than words are realized examples that demonstrate expectations for approval. In the case of completion standards, you should compile examples of each approval stage as a reference point for the team to refer to. Ideally, you want an example for each type of content type. Some examples of this would be:

- *Player locomotion*

- *Player action*

- *Enemy locomotion*

- *Enemy action*

- *Cinematic*

- *In-Game Scripted Event*

- *NPC action*

Being able to show examples of each type at each stage of completion will give the team clear examples of what is required for something to be approved at each step. It will also encourage them to show progress, as the early stages require it. The more people can see work being approved in earlier stages at different levels of completion, the more the team will naturally grow.

Conditional Approvals

Instead of a binary approval state, it can be valuable to have conditional approval states. Especially for more complex features or shots, conditional approvals allow for the work to move to the next completion standard. What this looks like in practice is:

- *Blue Feedback – Further discussion is required during the next phase to align feedback*

- *Purple Feedback – Feedback needs to be addressed to pass the next CS approval*

- *Red Feedback – Feedback needs to be addressed to pass current CS approval*

With this sort of conditional feedback, it requires the approver to internally prioritize the importance of the feedback they are providing. And it gives the person receiving the feedback the chance to process and prioritize the feedback they need to address.

It is important here to make sure there is accountability around this conditional feedback being addressed. Which means having a place where feedback is tracked across the approval process so that it can be easily referred to is important and necessary to establish.

Including Production, Quality Verification and User Research

As you add more process, structure and complexity to the approval process, it becomes more necessary to include and rely upon your production and QV partners. Clearly, when it comes to tracking feedback and approvals, production partners should have best practices that can align across disciplines and that all exist within a 'source of truth.' Which means a single place that either houses all of the feedback information within itself or is a hub that links to all of the feedback so that it can be easily found. And depending on the tools or tracking software used, this could feed into the scope and tracking workflows.

As for QV partners, it is worth discussing how they can or should be part of the approval process. Is there a specific work or completion standard that should include QV testing to validate that it is able to be reviewed or approved? At what completion standard should something be flagged as ready to be tested and bugs filed? What are the types of bugs you would like QV to prioritize in terms of aesthetics or game feel? All of these are conversations you should have with QV partners once the team has created examples of each content type.

The additional benefit that can come from including production and QV partners in the review and approval process is that it can give everyone a shared vocabulary between feedback and bug descriptions. For instance, the term 'twitch' can have multiple meanings across disciplines. It can speak to hyper-responsiveness when applied to game feel. It can mean a fidget or idle breaker when applied to the name of an action. Or it can be a motion element, adding a fast micro-movement to the animation as an intentional choice. It is just as likely to be a bug description that may be used to describe a bad blend or 'pop' in the IK. Including representatives from each group can help to unify the vocabulary, which can make for a smoother post-production and finagling process.

This can then naturally carry over to how user research and player testing engage with animation needs and feedback. Having a clear set of priorities and a vocabulary of feedback for members of the team outside of animation means that playtest sessions can also be used as a way of validating choices and decisions in terms of style and feel. It can also create a communication process that will become increasingly valuable in the later stages of production, as we will discuss later in this chapter.

Communicating Approvals

When something is approved, it is important and valuable to communicate that to the team. It shows concrete progress, which every team appreciates. It is a positive sense of accomplishment for the person having the work approved. And it signals downstream teams that they are free and clear to do the work they need to accomplish. Approvals are something worth celebrating.

What is important here is having a consistent place to track and communicate micro and macro approvals to the appropriate team members. Spamming a communication channel that includes the entire project with every approval of every completion standard can quickly become noise and turn the celebration of completion into something performative. In those cases, communicating big approvals, like firsts of a content type or full completion, is an appropriate cadence to notify the entire team. For every other approval, having a more targeted approval communication channel focused on those most directly involved is likely the best place for that to come across as a signal, not noise.

SHARED LIBRARIES

Once you have approved work, one of the biggest gifts that continues to pay off is a shared library of references, poses and animations that the team has full access to. This works to give both regularly available examples of what finished work looks like as well as inspiration for what the possibility space is. This is really the ultimate realization of the reference from the vision documentation and approved final quality animations. But there are some valuable points to keep in mind in the curation of these libraries.

Reference Videos

This will likely start with the reference videos you and the team found while defining and realizing the animation vision. But it shouldn't stop there. Throughout the project, as you find references that match the tone or vision, those should be added to the library as inspiration. Likewise, any general reference to physicality or acting is worth adding to the library. Especially when it comes to different animals, there can never be too much reference available for the team.

However, too much reference can be almost worthless if it isn't organized well. Luckily, taxonomy exists for these very sorts of reasons.[2] Thinking of your reference library as a hierarchy of groups, starting macro then micro, can give a clear and natural approach towards organizing the reference library. Like a well thought out naming structure or project file structure, this can allow you to add more reference groups while still allowing for ease of searching (Figure 11.2).

Pose and Motion Libraries

Like with reference libraries, you should be collecting all manner of poses and actions that the team can easily reference and use in their own work. This can provide consistency in both quality and style, as well as empower faster workflows, both in blocking out actions and applying finishing touch details.

For pose libraries, beyond shared idle poses most often used for gameplay, it is valuable to have specific libraries for hands and faces. Both can take time to individually craft appealing poses and expressions. So with a library of poses that the team can immediately apply and then tweak, the process of creating more appealing and consistent hand and facial animation can happen much faster and with more consistency (Figures 11.3 and 11.4).

Something to keep in mind in regards to hand poses is that not all hand poses mean the same thing in different cultures.[3] So depending on where your character is from or where your game is likely to be sold, you should take into account the hand gestures being created and used. And if you are making a multi-cultural cast of characters, labeling different hand gestures as specifically offensive in different cultures is a good habit to get into.

FIGURE 11.2   An example of a reference library taxonomy chart.

You can even take those facial pose libraries and turn them into fully animated expressions, as I discussed in the *Animating an Agent of Mayhem*[4] talk I presented at GDC in 2017. Which leads to motion libraries in general.

Motion libraries can exist in many different forms. Some are legacy databases of every animation that a studio has created. Some are a library of all motion capture data the studio has captured. Some are specifically curated or captured to include basic, general-purpose motions that can be used to quickly prototype or pre-visualize features or scenes. Like with reference libraries, organization here is the key. A taxonomic approach is

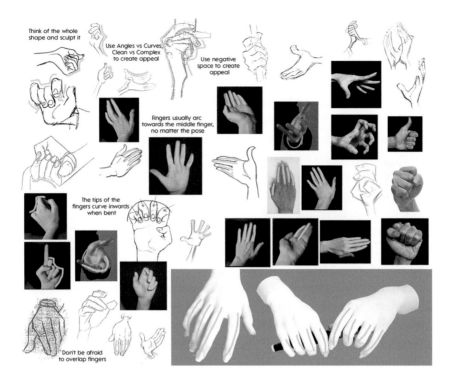

FIGURE 11.3   A hand pose style guide I have used to inform hand pose libraries I have made.

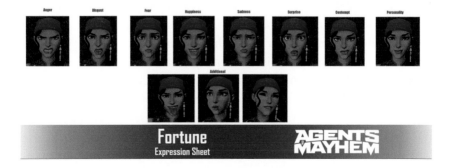

FIGURE 11.4   A facial pose style guide used on *Agents of Mayhem* to inform Fortune's facial expression library.

certainly beneficial here, but it is important to think even a step past that. Being able to tag and track the data through naming structures and/or meta-data is incredibly important for people to then find the specific type of motion data they are looking for. The tricky part here is how to actually classify the motions with the right kind of information.

As libraries get bigger, searching for something as simple as a kick can quickly become a time-consuming task. Do you want a forward kick, a side kick or a backflip with a kick? How many of those qualifiers have been labeled in that file? Now what if you want to search for a kick with certain gameplay metrics, like a kick that keeps the character in place or has them translate forward 2 meters during the action? This is also nothing to say about the performance of the action itself. Should the person be kicking like it is an effortless motion or one with a lot of effort and heft behind it? And what rig was any of this originally captured or authored on? Did it have correlating facial captures? What is the quality level of the data? The more files you have, the more time it will take to look at and assess each individual file. If it takes longer to find the motions than it would to block them out, the value of having this large library diminishes with the addition of each new file.

And that is all in terms of finding the action you are looking for explicitly in terms of creating something new. There are likely contractual reasons in place around what data can or cannot be used in terms of specific characters, actors and projects. Which makes the ability to track by actor, artist, project and date not only a legal best practice but also an important one in making sure future use of data can be properly attributed to the people involved in its existence.

The best way to do all of this at scale is not one I have an easy answer for. It almost certainly involves trained taxonomists, archivists and data managers to inform best practices. Using a shared language on how to describe the motions, either through something like Laban Movement Analysis or Desmond Morris' dictionary of actions, would certainly be beneficial. And it will almost certainly involve machine learning as both a method to identify and catalogue, but also as a motivator for having these databases available for training the AI models it uses to generate motion. But the choices we all individually make in terms of how we track, attribute and build the methods and tools used for this will have an impact with long-lasting ripples on how animation and performances are created in the future.

ITERATION AND CHANGE REQUESTS

Everything up to this point has been in a rather orderly, perfect world scenario of everything going out as planned. That is rarely, if ever, going to be the case. There are going to be changes in direction based on external feedback, changes in leadership or best laid plans simply not working out as intended. This is the true test of the vision and processes that have been established. Whether the changes required are large or small, they can bring tension and ripple further than anyone expected. Which is why it is a good practice to have a process for engaging with this sort of feedback, which can be applied to smaller and larger scale changes. And as an example, I am going to show how this was used to adapt to a change of direction in *Dragon Age*. Considering this book has been about building and communicating an intentional, cross-disciplinary vision, that is the scale of change best represented here. But it should also be clear how this can scale to any size of change required at a macro or micro level.

Identify Problem Statements

The first step to responding to late-stage feedback is to clarify the actual problem that needs to be addressed. This is an effort towards defining an objective statement that gets to the problem that needs to be answered. Like with the other approaches outlined in this book, the best way to start defining anything is with questions.

- *What is the player experience issue we are trying to solve?*
- *What is the impact if we maintain the current course?*

These questions can get everyone to think at the same level of specificity, when some may tend to approach these problems at either to low or high of a level in their perception of what needs to be solved. In other words, as with other parts of the process, start first by defining the Function that needs to be addressed before jumping to the Form.

If you have a feedback process in place with the QV and UXR teams, then the answers to those questions are more likely to be presented as part of the feedback itself. That will also mean you are less likely to be surprised by new feedback, as generally issues found there are not unknown, but the priority and severity of the issue can change as more people engage with the creation. What is less easy to mitigate are changes to another discipline's vision or direction that impact the core intent of the animation vision.

As discussed in Chapter 6, at the core of the player's animation vision in *Dragon Age* was the identity of the factions. The narrative, art and design vision to have those be core choices was what informed the movement elements defining the animation. This meant there was no impact on the animation vision by removing individual factions or changing any specific weapon type within a faction or its specific weapon hold. The result of this flexibility meant that as scope required fewer factions to be supported, animation could continue forward with the remaining faction visions, as they were all unique, self-contained and still matched the intent of faction being the first and foundational choice the player made. The problem only comes when a faction is moved from being the core choice to a secondary or tertiary choice. Which is precisely what happened, where the change requested was to have more traditional archetypes, or classes, be the core player choice, with factions then added as a secondary reflection or flavor to the experience. This obviously has implications across all disciplines, so a clear, objective problem statement is important here.

To properly understand how best to address this across the disciplines, we can apply the above questions.

- *What is the player experience issue we are trying to solve?*

  - *'What a faction means is not universally understood without some explanation. So as a first question it can be confusing.'*

- *What is the impact if we maintain the current course?*

  - *'Players, especially those new to the IP, may experience decision paralysis with this as their first choice. Which can lead to frustration as players may feel like they made a choice that doesn't match their intended playstyle or fantasy.'*

The project leadership decision was to then change from factions to the more traditional archetypes of Warrior, Rogue and Mage as the first choice the player makes. But still include factions as a choice, to be reflected in the experience where possible. Which then leads to the problem statement in response to this change being, *'The player needs to feel that their choice of class archetype is core to their experience.'* With this understood, we can all move on to the next step of the process.

Identify Constraints

Once the problem has been properly identified, it is most often the case that people want to move directly to finding solutions. But that is jumping the gun, and the further along in the development cycle a team is, the more of a problem it can become. When projects are still early, the ability to adjust to proposed solutions is easier. But once foundations have been laid and structures are in place, solutions that cause changes can fundamentally alter what is being built. This is why, regardless of the phase of the project, the next step of the process should be for the different disciplines to list out their constraints within the problem space. It could be tech, time or creative. Big or small. It is important to remember and convey that constraints are not a bad thing. Like when defining both performances and style, constraints are a wonderful tool in helping to focus the solution space. They also allow different disciplines to learn and not assume what the actual constraints are. As often, they can be different than the perceived ones.

Once established, those constraints should be prioritized so that everyone understands how important each of those constraints is. Some may be objectively prohibitive in terms of time and tech. Some may be more subjective, based on taste, tone and style. Both are valuable as they clarify where people's natural bias tends to be and again align the team with what is driving the constraints. All of this helps to cut through what teams perceive as the reason behind constraints and the reality of why those constraints exist.

While having these conversations can take time, the more reliably everyone engages with this step, the more it becomes internalized as everyone better understands the needs and biases of their team members. This means the time required on this step and the one before it will become less and less as trust and understanding of problems and constraints become more shared across the team.

In the case of the change from factions to archetypes, the constraints of the different disciplines varied across objective and subjective constraints. Though the most consistent and highest priority constraint was immediately obvious as the need to continue using as much of the already-created work as possible. With that major constraint defined, along with the high-level problem statement to make sure the choice of archetypes was meaningful, it was time to discuss solutions.

List Possible Solutions

Now is the time to brainstorm all of the possible solutions. Or, in other terms, ideas on how to assign Form to the Function. The best brainstorming sessions should allow for every possible solution to be presented without judgement. Let both the conscious and unconscious, creative mind flow and add everything being presented to a list.

It can be valuable for someone to keep track of which constraints the possible solutions are most in conflict with as they are being listed out. Though this can also be done after the brainstorm session. What is more important is that the constraints, big and small, are assigned to the solutions at some point. This will help when a decision needs to be made, as you can then compare the priorities of the different solutions to which is most doable or least problematic. It also allows team members to see that their constraints and concerns are being considered. Which then results in an awareness that mitigating or overcoming those constraints should be a priority for any solution.

Dismissing or shying away from conversations around the impact of those constraints in regards to decided-upon solutions is a common cause of frustration and tension across teams. Being able to engage in constraints allows for trust and respect to build across teams. That is the continued value of the first two steps of this process. When problem-solving starts at this solution-focused step, issues of consistency of vision and prioritization can quickly become arbitrary and reactive to the moment. The more a team is in a reactive state, the more likely they are to miss things and burn themselves out.

Returning to the example of changing from factions to archetypes, here is what listing possible solutions and constraints looked like.

- *Possible Solution: Adapt more legacy assets from previous games*

  - *Reasoning*

    - *May provide a more closely aligned vision of the archetypes without starting from scratch*

  - *Constraint Conflicts*

    - *Not a 1:1 match in terms of quality, style and function of existing work*

- *Possible Solution: Remove the differentiation of faction and archetype styles*

  - *Reasoning*

    - *Allows for maximum amounts of mixing and matching of created work*

- *Constraint Conflicts*

  - *Each faction vision was pushed to be unique in style and tone, which can look and feel like a mismatch when applied in an arbitrary manner.*

  - *The core choice is not visually represented in a clear and meaningful way*

- *Possible Solution: Adapt faction and archetype vision to best suit the needs of each discipline*

  - *Reasoning*

    - *Allows for the most flexibility based on the current state of each discipline*

  - *Constraint Conflicts*

    - *A connected sense of vision across disciplines will be diminished*

From the possible solutions presented on their own, any seem reasonable at first glance. But with the constraint conflicts listed, it becomes readily apparent that the third option best meets the needs of the problem statement while taking into account the core constraint agreed upon by the team. Without the first two steps in this process, had those other solutions been the ones mandated, the impact could have had a much more serious impact across the team.

Test for Success

Once a solution is decided upon, clearly defining how you can test and prove what success looks like is key. This gives people an objective truth to build towards and assigns accountability in terms of realizing the solution. Often, what this entails is how the solution overcomes or fits within constraints. But before a proposed solution is communicated to the team or can be considered successful, a clear goal and objective of what success looks like need to be established. This can be an expectation of a playable prototype to prove the solution. Or maybe the creation of a new tool that overcomes the constraint. It may be that a clear completion standard process needs to be agreed upon, which then requires the solution to go through the associated review and approval process. Depending on the scale and impact of the change, the requirements of what is needed to validate success are no less important than anything else being reviewed and approved on the project.

What this looked like for the animation vision of *Dragon Age* was that assigning specific faction aesthetics to archetypes was straightforward in two out of three instances. The Warrior and Grey Warden were a natural fit, which was great since that was the furthest along at the time. Having the Mage use the Shadow Dragon vision allowed that unique movement style, as well as the very specific data we captured, to still be used. The Rogue was the single instance of not having a clear one-to-one analogue, as the desire to use specific weapons was a mix of work already established for the Antivan Crows and Veil Jumpers. So a return to the movement elements, specifically adapting to the archetype, was necessary here (Figure 11.5).

When visually mapping out how all of these related to one another, it immediately became clear what elements needed to be adjusted for the Rogue. Using the Antivan Crow as the core vision was closest, so that would be the core, with a slight adjustment to lean into more still moments instead of always being active. And to allow for more of the Veil Jumper-style animations to better fit, the push to bring in some more of the fluid aspects of Chinese martial arts was important. This ultimately led to the player archetype visions being:

- *War Drum WARRIOR*

- *Hip-Hop MAGE*

- *Ballerina Kung Fu ROGUE*

	High	Low	Broad	Contained	Fluid	Staccato	Still	Active	Effort	Effortless	
Rogue (Crow)	1	0	1	0	1	0	0	1	0	1	1x Warrior Overlap, 3x Mage Overlap
Warrior	1	0	0	1	0	1	1	0	1	0	1x Rogue Overlap, 1x Mage Overlap
Mage	0	1	1	0	0	1	0	1	0	1	1x Warrior Overlap, 3x Rogue Overlap
							CAUTION		CAUTION		

	High	Low	Broad	Contained	Fluid	Staccato	Still	Active	Effort	Effortless	
Rogue (Veil)	0	1	0	1	0	1	1	0	1	0	4x Warrior Overlap, 2x Mage Overlap
Warrior	1	0	0	1	0	1	1	0	1	0	4x Rogue Overlap, 1x Mage Overlap
Mage	0	1	1	0	0	1	0	1	0	1	2x Rogue Overlap, 1x Warrior Overlap
					DANGER		CAUTION		CAUTION		

	High	Low	Broad	Contained	Fluid	Staccato	Still	Active	Effort	Effortless	
Rogue	1	0	1	0	1	0	1	0	0	1	2x Warrior Overlap, 2x Mage Overlap
Warrior	1	0	0	1	0	1	1	0	1	0	2x Rogue Overlap, 1x Mage Overlap
Mage	0	1	1	0	0	1	0	1	0	1	2x Rogue Overlap, 1x Warrior Overlap

FIGURE 11.5 A chart that maps out how each movement element matches each archetype. And how trying to use any existing faction style one to one on the rogue presented vision issues in regards to the other archetypes.

This vision allowed us to reuse a lot of work that had been done and add our own unique vision to traditional archetypes, which allows for the choice of each to both look and feel distinct to players.

Which ultimately shows that paying specific attention to how feedback is structured and addressed allows for more creative control and better decision-making across an entire team. It can help you move out of a reactive state of perceived needs and biases and towards a proactive approach that builds trust and respect. And that is the core of what makes for the best teams and creative work.

NOTES

1 Two specific game dev-related resources I would suggest in terms of understanding different feedback approaches across different disciplines are the 2021 book *A Playful Production Process: For Game Designers (and Everyone)* by Richard Lemarchand and the 2012 GDC talk *Concrete Practices to Be a Better Leader: Framing and Intent* by Brian Sharp.

2 Forgive the following tangent and indulgence, but I would be remiss to not mention my love of taxonomy to answer the silly question of what defines a sandwich. I will save linking my chart here, but when applying the taxonomy of sandwiches to the 'compliment sandwich' style of feedback, it actually makes that feedback approach much more valid. For instance, how much of a compliment to give can be based on the form itself (stacked, flat, wrapped, hinged) the thickness and substance of the form, and the type (sweet, savory, crunchy, soft). And that can be crafted in relation to how much of the substantive feedback inside should also be expected to be digested. Each person will have their own preference, but if you think of each person on your team as having a favorite sandwich type, then I can fully endorse the 'compliment sandwich.' I will stop myself here, as I could likely write a second book by diving deep into this ridiculous rabbit hole.

3 The approach to studying humans that Desmond Morris focused his career on is a wealth of knowledge and learnings in terms of how people communicate through motion and body language. Both the book *People Watching: The Desmond Morris Guide to Body Language* (2012) and the documentary series *The Human Animal* (1994) are well worth your time.

4 It feels a bit odd referencing myself, especially after directly sharing specifics of this talk in Chapter 6, but in terms of using facial expressions as a pose library and as a runtime system, I outline the approach in my 2017 GDC talk, *Animating an Agent of Mayhem*. Having you watch those in video is easier than me trying to explain here through text and images.

CHAPTER 12

Empowering the Team

EVERYTHING UP TO THIS point has been largely focused on either process or product. But at the heart of everything are the people. By starting with expectations, it put the people first as much as it did the product. But it is important to recognize that what really sets your project apart are the people on the team. Their specific sensibilities are what ultimately power and realize the vision. So it is important that we come full circle and finish where we started. By talking about the people.

By this point, it should be clear that my approach and sensibilities towards direction are not to erase the finger prints left by everyone touching the project but to make sure everyone on the team is working on something that can benefit from their unique finger prints. Learning what excites people and finding a place they can unleash that excitement is one of the greatest joys of being a director. What follows are some various approaches and experiences I have found to have significant value towards empowering and unleashing a team's full potential.

ESTABLISHING VALUES

At the core of every person is a set of values. These values drive priorities and decision-making. If logic and reason are what drive the head, values are often informed by the heart and help to drive the gut. Which means understanding and establishing values is a natural extension of establishing expectations. And the best tool I have found for this is a Values Worksheet, recommended to me by Simon Unger. The instructions are in

DOI: 10.1201/9781003356196-12

the sheet itself, which is included here as a visual reference, along with the full sheet in the online resource pack (Figures 12.1 and 12.2).

And to see it in practice, I offer my own answers. It is important to note that these can vary based on context and time. In terms of context, because this is for members of a team working on a collaborative project, it is important to state that their values should be in terms of the project, team and work place. The values people have there can be different than if they were to approach this with the mindset of their personal lives. Which makes sense because the expectations and experiences of the two are likely to vary.

I also like to keep different versions of this sheet, as I see the top values fluctuate depending on the phase or state of the project and the team I am working with. While the ten values I mark are largely consistent, the priority of the top three feels like adjustments to the headspace I am currently occupying. Which makes this worth revisiting every 6 months or so to check in on where your values are at (Figure 12.3).

Where this becomes valuable, beyond self-reflection, is seeing what other members of the team prioritize as their values. What you will find is that a lot of miscommunications or competing priorities across team members or the project can happen across these value lines. This allows you to reframe conversations in terms of what people naturally value, which helps you not get frustrated with a person but better understand what is in their heart and driving their gut.

It can be valuable to have a place where team members can post and update their values for the team to refer to. Though something like this can be personal for people, it is important to make posting these sorts of things as optional, not required.

INTERESTS AND INFLUENCES

Another insight into what influences the heart of the team is learning more about their specific interests and influences. Creating collages of different interests and influences can be a great activity and opportunity for team members to show what creatively excites them. Anything from music, movies, games, activities, books, food or trips, there is no limit to what people can include here. There can be as many or as few references as people want to include. The intent is for people to step back, think about what inspires them and then display it in a format that other people can see.

VALUES CLARIFICATION

Knowing our values helps us to make correct decisions in our lives.
Knowing other's values helps us to support one another in ways that matter
most to each individual. It should be retaken on a yearly basis.

From the list below, **select ten of the values you consider most important to you**
at this time. Add others that are not on the list. No particular order. Just choose ten.

_____ ACHIEVEMENT (sense of accomplishment)
_____ ADVANCEMENT ("moving up the ladder")
_____ ADVENTURE (new, challenging experiences)
_____ AUTONOMY (working independently)
_____ CHALLENGE (stimulates full use of potential)
_____ CLEANLINESS
_____ COOPERATIVE (teamwork)
_____ COMPASSION
_____ CREATIVITY (being imaginative, innovative)
_____ ECONOMIC SECURITY (having enough money)
_____ FAMILY HAPPINESS
_____ FRIENDSHIP (close relationship with others)
_____ FREEDOM (absence of restraints)
_____ GENEROSITY (willingness to give freely)
_____ HEALTH (mind, body and spirit)
_____ HUMOR
_____ INDEPENDENCE (self-reliant)
_____ INTEGRITY (honesty, sincerity)
_____ INNER HARMONY (at peace with one self)
_____ KNOWLEDGE (understanding gained through study and experience)
_____ LOYALTY
_____ LEADERSHIP
_____ LOVE (unconditional, caring)
_____ NON-VIOLENCE (in thought, word and deed)
_____ PEACE
_____ PERSONAL TIME (sufficient time for self/other interests)
_____ PLEASURE
_____ POWER (authority)
_____ RESPONSIBILITY (accountable for results)
_____ RECOGNITION (acknowledgement)
_____ SERVICE (helping others)
_____ SECURITY
_____ SPIRITUALITY
_____ STATUS (position viewed to be important)
_____ SURRENDER TO THE DIVINE
_____ TRUTHFULNESS (in thought, word and deed)
_____ WEALTH (strong financial means)
_____ WISDOM (understanding based on accumulation of learning)
_____
_____

FIGURE 12.1   The first page of the values worksheet.

VALUES CLARIFICATION FORM - PRIORITY GRID

1. Insert the items to be prioritized, in any order, in Section A.
2. Compare two items at a time, circling the one you prefer in Secion B.
   Do not think heaviliy, rather go with your first 'gut feeling.' Trust your instincts.
3. Count the number of times each item was circled - Place that number in the small box at Section C.
   Note that the grid runs both horizontal and vertical as the numbers increase. Each number has nine comparisons.
4. If two items are circled the same number of times, look back to Section B to compare again and give the one
   you most prefer another half point.(.5)
5. Once you have your order of preference, list the top three in Section D.

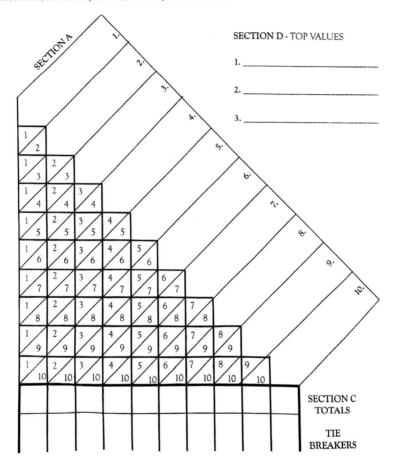

FIGURE 12.2   The second page of the values worksheet.

These are also perfect candidates to post in a place other members of the team can view and engage with. Creating a 'Meet the Team' page or resource that has these collages, along with the above values and more traditional information like project responsibilities, can help to show a more complete picture of the team. It can also start conversations among

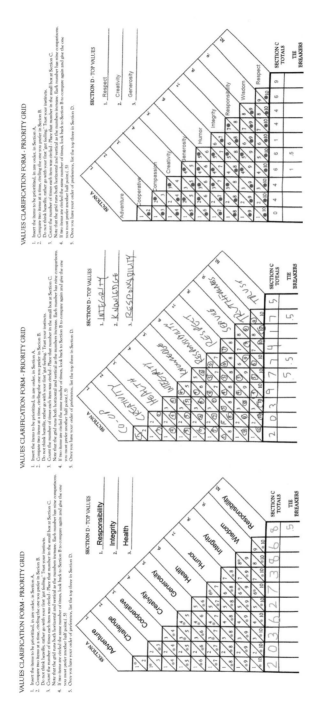

FIGURE 12.3   Different versions of my results of the worksheet, showing how priorities can vary over time and across different teams.

FIGURE 12.4   My personal collage of interests and influences.

team members with shared interests that they may not have realized they had. More than once, I have seen teammates that rarely talked bond over shared interests they saw on one another's collages, which leads to each feeling more seen and connected. It can also give new team members an opportunity to get to know people and get a sense of the different interests and personalities on the team (Figure 12.4).

FOSTERING CREATIVITY AND CONNECTIONS

As an extension of the team's interests and influences, you should always be on the lookout for opportunities to expand shared or especially relevant inspirations into team-wide experiences. These are direct ways to influence team culture, morale and the overall creative choices on the project itself. Something like the 'Dragon Age: Love Connection' as discussed in Chapter 8 would fall into this category. Team outings focused on learning or experiencing skills required for the game, such as learning how to properly fire a bow, playing a sport, learning to dance or taking an improv class, would be more traditional examples of this. But it can go even further than that. Here are some specific examples from teams I have led in the past.

During my time at Volition, one of the technical animators on the team was talking about a holiday tradition of Parranda, that takes place in Puerto Rico. The way he explained it was that it was like caroling but not leaving a house until they gave you food or drinks and then joined in to go to the next house. This would go on all night, as essentially everyone in the community would then be outside together, eating, drinking and having a good time. As he was talking about it, another team member who spent some time in Puerto Rico ran in to say how much he loved Parranda. Seeing the opportunity to bring a tradition they loved as a bonding experience for the team, I pitched the idea of having a Parranda-style studio event.

What this meant in practice was learning about the specific food, drinks and music most associated with Parranda and finding a core group of people within the studio that would make up the core of the group that would start the event. Each room in the studio had a gift box of food and drinks placed in it. And then, at a specified time, with the encouragement of studio leadership, the core group came together with all manner of instruments and would travel room to room throughout the studio, playing music and bringing people along as they shared the food and drinks from their room. It culminated with the majority of the studio dancing, singing, eating and drinking in the lobby on a random weekday in July. While this clearly disrupted a day of work and had no direct tie to anything the team was working on, the result was a boost to team morale and a stronger general energy and connection to one another. Which may not be easy to quantify, but the value of those experiences is long-lasting.

A bit more directly tied to the goals of a project were the Good Bad Movie viewings I held for the *Dragon Age* animation team. With the updated vision of boldly reflecting choice and intent, it became clear that leaning into the sensibilities of 'B-Movies' could help break the team out of thinking in more established fantasy tropes. As well as showing examples of creations that wore their heart on their sleeve, even if the execution was spotty. The approach was to start with some of my personal favorite 'bad movies' and then take suggestions from the team. The cadence was about once a month, with the time and movie voted on by the team. As new team members would join, we would set up a 'Good Bad Movie' viewing as part of their welcome to the team experience. As we talked more about the movies during work hours, members of other disciplines would toss out suggestions and join in on the viewings. It also became an unofficial recruitment tool, as I would post the movies in an ongoing thread on Twitter. Several people would mention during interviews that one of the things that made them interested in joining the team was the clear sense of camaraderie on display.

While all of this can feel frivolous or unnecessary to the actual work required for a project, this really embodies philosopher and critic Mikhail Bahktin's idea of *carnival* or *folk festivities*. They bring people together, cutting through a studio's socio-hierarchical divides, to encourage a natural sense of frivolity, laughter and connection. So many elements of a project, studio, company or corporation build up positions of power and distance over time. These sorts of *folk festivities* are liberating forces, and as proposed by Bahktin, 'laughing truth … degrades power.'[1]

It is important to understand how all of this influences the culture of the team. And that your choices here have an outweighing impact on influencing the culture. Culture can be a great way to pull people together, but it can also make other people on the team feel like an outsider.[2] Find opportunities for everyone on the team to drive team activities in an effort to diversify the team culture. The interest and influence collages can be a great place to start by asking if team members would like to demonstrate one of their areas of interest with the rest of the team. This can give them an opportunity to share something they are enthusiastic about, but it can also open up the entire team to a new area of expertise to research and creatively draw from.

MANAGING FOR GROWTH

While the majority of this book has been focused on realizing a creative vision more than people management, there is a key part of being a manager that every director should take into account, even if that is not a required, core part of the job responsibilities. And that means helping to chart and mentor the growth of each team member. As mentioned in the forward of this book, clear career growth and mentorship directly contribute to higher job satisfaction, work/life balance and trust in leadership. Which means the more you prioritize and support this for any team you are directing, the stronger the team will be. Which will then further push the realization of the animation and project vision.

One method I have found to be incredibly valuable in terms of giving clarity to the expectations of a job role and how to grow to the next level, is a Job Role Matrix. The way this works is that across the top of a sheet, you list out the levels of expertise for a job role. A common example may be:

- Associate

- Mid-Level

- Senior

- Principal

Then, down the left side of the sheet would be the areas of expertise required for the role. In terms of animators, this could be areas like:

- Concepting

- Aesthetics

- Workflows

- Implementation

- Collaboration

Then, across each cell of the sheet, you plot out the expectations for each area of expertise across each level of experience for the role. There is an example of this in the supplemental materials on the book's website, which you can reference and modify to your team and studio needs (Figure 12.5). Notice as well that the track of craft creator versus craft director, or leadership, is separated. It is important to offer opportunities for career growth that extend beyond moving into leadership roles, as being the best in your craft does not always equate to being the best in a leadership role. Not everyone will even want to move into a leadership role, but if the only opportunity for career growth and higher compensation comes from taking on leadership roles, then that is where people will be incentivized to take on and not let go, even if it isn't a good fit. Instead, it is better to create two tracks, with the craft creator roles focused on the depth of their impact as opposed to the craft leadership roles, which are more focused on the breadth of their impact. Just be aware that the breadth of impact is naturally noticed by more people, especially those in the roles that often control budgets and compensation. So it will be your responsibility to highlight the depth of impact as being just as important, valuable and in need of proper compensation.

I was lucky enough in 2020 to help craft an updated version of the Job Role Matrix for EA with a handful of other animation directors within the organization. The process was incredibly valuable in thinking about and talking through what goes into a role at various levels of expertise across different studios and projects. The act of breaking down the required areas

Craft Creation Career Path	Associate Animator II	Animator I	Animator II	Senior Animator I	Senior Animator II	Principal Animator
Craft Direction Career Path	N/A	N/A	Lead Specialization Available	Associate Animation Director	Animation Director	Senior Animation Director
	Developing Summary: Operates effectively with frequent, detailed direction and mentorship Demonstrates ability for high quality asset creation with potential to row Proficient in 1 or more areas of craft.	Doing Summary: • Works effectively with frequent direction • Demonstrates mastery of craft in several specific areas • Creates content following established benchmark; • Handles mid-complexity tasks • Influencial at individual task and peer level	Owning Summary: • Works effectively with high-level direction • Demonstrates broad craft mastery • Consistently creates content following established benchmark • Owns/leads mid-scale complexity tasks	Leading (team or by example) Summary: • Capable of work largely self-directed • Demonstrates best-in-class craft mastery and expert knowledge • Operates proactively and with big picture thinking • Owns/leads broad complexity tasks	Driving (project-wide influence) Summary: • Influences project/team across all disciplines/features • Works on complex tasks with multiple dependencies and interconnections • Works on items that have an impact across the entire game, and/or the most complex/largest areas of the	Driving (studio-wide influence) Summary: • Sets direction for the craft forward across the studio (e.g. large team, studio, or franchise) • Focused on high impact, strategic initiatives to drive the products and craft forward.
GENERAL CAPABILITIES						
CONCEPTING *'Matching Function & Form'* Prototyping Reference Gathering Pre-vis Look Dev System Planning	**Appreciates** how the craft of animation overlaps with game design, art, narrative and engineering to fulfill pre-vis objectives. **Plans, shoots, acts out, and gathers** individual reference materials. **Creates** individual Animation assets as **defined** by more senior members of the team to fulfill pre-vis objectives. Breaks down and details the needs of **small** sized work.	• **Understands** how the craft of animation overlaps with game design, art, narrative and engineering to fulfill pre-vis objectives. • Plans, shoots, acts out and gathers reference materials **for features to fullfill pre-vis objectives.** • **Creates** individual Animation assets to fulfill pre-vis objectives. • Breaks down and details the needs of **small to medium** sized work.	• **Actively applies** the craft of animation alongside game design, art and engineering to fulfill pre-vis objectives. • Contributes to **oversight of reference** that fulfills pre-vis objectives. • **Plans individual animation systems** to fulfill pre-vis objectives with oversight from more senior team members. • Breaks down and details the needs of **medium to large** sized work.	Senior Animator I • **Expertly executes** the craft of animation alongside game design, art, narrative and engineering to fulfill pre-vis objectives. • **Define reference** for multiple features as aligned with the Director's vision. • **Plans and oversees** individual animation systems to fulfill pre-vis objectives. • Breaks down and details the needs of **large** sized work. Associate Animation Director • Works with Director to **define the overlap** of animation, game design, art and engineering to fulfill pre-vis objectives. • **Provides high level consultation**, and champions pre-vis objectives and visual targets in relation to player experience as defined by Directors. • Works directly with the Animation Director and relevant disciplines to **establish and hone in the feature lists**.	Senior Animator II • **Plans and oversees multiple animation or cinematic needs** to fulfill pre-vis objectives. Animation Director • **Defines the overlap** of animation, game design, art and engineering, and **guides** the animation team to fulfill pre-vis objectives. • **Sets vision** for pre-vis objectives by establishing and presenting the project's unique animation identity via direction, style, and tone. • **Holistically curates and presents** reference materials for the entire project. Supports and guides team to deliver content to fulfill vision. • **Consults** on consumer motivations for playing the game/genre and partners with EP and Brand directors to reflect the vision of the player experience.	Principal Animator • **Innovates** new animation systems and concepts to fulfill pre-vis objectives. Senior Animation Director • **Drives unique vision** across projects by establishing the studio's unique animation identity. • Holistically curates and presents reference materials to **set the foundation for an entire studio.** • **Supports and guides** the visions of Animation Direction across their studio. • Ensures teams have exposure and access to industry trends and tech to **fulfill their studio vision.** • **Actively** makes educated decisions in reference to **data/telemetry driven objectives** across studio products. • **Seeks out** consumer motivations for playing the game/genre and partners with EP and Brand directors **to implement the vision** that
AESTHETICS *'Execution of the Form'* Principles of Animation Quality Consistency Character Portrayal Physicality and Action Animation Turnaround Time	Delivers content that demonstrates a **solid** understanding of animation principles, physicality, and acting, applied **consistently** on individual animation clips. **Adjusts** their work to the specific style and tone of the project.	• Delivers content that demonstrates a **solid** understanding of animation principles, applied consistently on **specific types of content.** • Executes and delivers content that is consistent with **specific feature** aesthetics. • Executes on acting/emotional portrayal within **one or more** character performances. • Adjusts to the specific style and tone of the project, and **develops** their ability to work in **various styles**. • Actively **seeks out** peer feedback	• Delivers content that demonstrates an **expert** understanding of animation principles, applied consistently across the game, on **any type of content.** • Executes and delivers content that is consistent with **the game** aesthetic. • Executes on acting principles and emotional portrayal within **several character** performances. • Expertly adjusts to implement the specific tone and style of the project **in all situations**, and showcases adaptability to **various styles.** • Actively seeks out peer feedback and ensures **effective turnaround time** for Director feedback	Senior Animator I • Expertly understands and delivers content that is used as a **quality benchmark** for various features and scenes. • Demonstrates extensive experience animating in various styles, and **contributes to setting** the Animation style and tone for the project. • **Provides feedback** to junior team members and actively **reinforces** the animation direction and philosophy – across the team. Associate Animation Director • Expert-level understanding and **communication** of Animation Principles across the team, in partnership with the animation director for **setting the aesthetic vision**. • Regularly **reviews** team animations and demonstrates experience in adapting **feedback** delivery to team members, achieving the vision set by Animation Direction on product segment.	Senior Animator II • Expertly understands, delivers, and pushes content that is used as a quality benchmark for the entire game – **improving established aesthetic conventions.** • Drives aesthetic execution, in specific areas of the product to be a **quality leading examples in their genre.** • Demonstrates extensive experience animating in various styles, and is a **key driver** to setting the Animation style and tone for the project. • Aids in making **aesthetic choices for the game** and actively reinforces the animation direction and philosophy. Animation Director • Establishes and guides **high level vision** across all domains and systems. • **Defines quality pillars** for the project, and **provides guidance and feedback** to animators and AADs on how to target, conform and	Principal Animator • Tackles the most complex and artistically-challenging tasks, while **pushing the quality bar within their studio.** • Displays a mastery in the pinciples of animation through delivery of content that serves as quality benchmark and inspiration **across their studio.** • Collaborates with other Director/s in **making aesthetic choices** for the game and actively reinforces the animation direction and philosophy **within their studio.** Senior Animation Director • Creates **exemplary** animation philosophies and direction, that **inspires and influences** other directors across other teams, studios or disciplines. • Defines or maintains **brand strategy** while providing catered guidance to other animation directors for achieving quality, within their studio, and overlaps their guidance to **multiple**

FIGURE 12.5 A portion of a Job Role Matrix for context of appearance. I recommend you read the supplemental version for full details.

of expertise and how those could naturally progress as someone becomes more experienced in their craft made a number of things clear.

The first is that everyone has a general sense of what the responsibilities of a role are, but when you need to be clearly descriptive of requirements, the specifics can be difficult and variable to define. And when discussing this with other directors, there is a lot of subjective experience based on the needs of specific projects that will certainly need to be taken into account. Workflows, tools and studio culture can all directly impact the priorities and needs of a job. Which is to say, no Job Role Matrix can be directly applied from one team or studio to another. The spirit and core may likely be consistent, but how that is directly defined and applied should be adapted to the needs of your team and studio. Establishing expectations here will directly impact the priorities of a role and help to either create more hyper-specialized and/or more well-rounded team members.

The next thing you will find, once you have a sheet like this in place, is that conversations around how someone is performing at their level become a lot more objective and consistent for each member of the team. You can directly talk about specific expectations a team member is meeting or exceeding and which areas they need to be given opportunities to grow in. This can help to inform direct areas of improvement as well as make a clear case as to why someone is ready for a promotion. All of this will help to keep you and the project leadership more honest about any unconscious bias you may have towards individual team members.

ONBOARDING NEW TEAM MEMBERS

As everything in this book has been about understanding, defining and communicating a direction for the team to realize, organizing a clear and consistent onboarding process for new team members should be rather straightforward. The order of events you took in the development of the direction has provided a robust map for new team members joining the project. What is really left, in regards to onboarding people to the direction and vision of the project, is establishing a clear and organized resource for people to find and follow the information. This is best suited as part of a wiki, or it could even be stored on a shared drive with an established folder structure.

The order of information I recommend largely mirrors the chapters in this book, but it is worth explaining the reason for each in a bit more detail.

1. *Animation Team*

2. *Animation Vision*

3. *Animation Production Practices*

4. *Animation Workflows*

5. *Animation Training*

Focusing on the animation team first is a subtle way of establishing that people come first. It allows those joining the team to get to know the people they will be working with and get a sense of the team values before the project needs them. This is the section where sharing the value work sheets, influence charts and any team creativity events (like our 'good bad movie' watch lists) are best suited. Though this focus on the people before the project is something that can and should be taken further. Whereas most studios I have worked on have made the focus of the onboarding process the project and getting new team members tasked as quickly as possible, Compulsion makes the focus of the onboarding process meeting team members. The first couple of weeks are scheduled to meet different people across the studio so that relationships can be formed in a way that isn't immediately transactional. The new team member is set up to have access to everything so that they can engage with the project at their own speed during those first couple of weeks. But the focus of people over the project, even during the onboarding process, is powerful in building trust and respect.

The animation vision as the second step in onboarding is meant to creatively inspire the new team member and convey a clear sense of direction for the project. All of this should be well and clearly documented and communicated by this point, so think of this as the final source of truth for that vision to exist. Start with the high-level vision presentation, but then have subpages or folders that go as in-depth as you like. Anything and everything vision-related should live here, but remember to keep it well organized. This is usually best organized by characters, style and features, though this will certainly vary based on the needs of the project.

Having production practices after the vision will help to establish that there is a clear understanding of what is needed to deliver on the vision. This should be where everything around completion standards, tracking sheets and the review and approval process should live. This is also the best place to link to other discipline production processes so that everyone has a clear sense of how they all link together.

While workflows have not been a focus of this book, this would be where documentation on the tools and tech used by the team. A lot of those are likely a mix of proprietary and new tools and tech, especially those defined by the unique tech needs of the project, as defined in Chapter 4. This can also be a good place to keep or link to the different pose, animation and reference libraries available to the team. One thing to keep in mind with this section is that this will almost certainly be the area that continues to grow during the course of the project. As new tech and tools are added to the workflow, documentation will also be required, which means this section is likely to not only grow but also have a number of different people growing it. Which means establishing a clear taxonomy and order for this section as soon as possible can be valuable. This will allow people to naturally sort their documentation into the appropriate areas, with less of a need to spend time curating and moving documentation throughout production. A good approach to start with here would be:

- First-Time Setup
  - Network
  - Software
- Project Structure
  - Naming Conventions
  - File Locations
- DCC
  - Rigs
  - Tools
- Runtime
  - Characters
  - Systems
    - Gameplay
    - Narrative

- Libraries
  - Pose
  - Animation
  - Reference

As discussed in Chapter 3, better workflows almost always result in better work. And easy access to the documentation of the tech and tools powering everything is a core part of those better workflows. Which makes the curation of this important to establish and maintain. Either by yourself or with the support of the team.

ASKING FOR HELP

Both from the start of this process and throughout, asking questions has been as important as providing answers. Which should hopefully make it easy for you to acknowledge when you don't know the answer. Because nothing demonstrates humility, trust and respect to those around you as saying, 'I don't know.' And few things are as destructive or stubborn as saying you do know something when it is clear that you don't. Saying 'I don't know' is never something to be ashamed of or embarrassed by. It is an opportunity to learn something new and ask for help from someone else on the team. And whenever someone in leadership is unafraid to ask for help, it demonstrates to everyone else on the team the ability to say they don't know.

One of the worst things that can happen to a team is when they are unwilling to admit gaps in their knowledge and try to make up for it with ego, bluster or dismissiveness. You surround yourself with experts so that you don't need to know all of the answers all the time. Your job is to know who to go to when you don't know an answer. And how to balance the needs of that answer against the creative vision and production realities of the project.

PASSING THE TORCH

This entire process should have made it clear that a vision and direction are not something you arbitrarily wield or demand. Leading a team is ultimately a collaborative effort, in which there are times you need to make decisions or point a way forward. The key is to know when to ask, when to listen and when to direct. Or, in the words of Craig Ferguson[3]:

1. *Does this need to be said?*

2. *Does this need to be said by me?*

3. *Does this need to be said by me now?*

Which all leads to the final step of being in a leadership position. Knowing when to step aside and give the opportunity to others. This is more than delegation, which hasn't been covered in this book, but is absolutely something you should be able to do with more ease when you have a more clearly communicated and intentional direction. No, this is about knowing when to give someone else the same opportunity to direct that you have been given.

The process of game development, when done well, is about passing the baton to the team member coming after you. By taking the time and care to understand the project vision, those ahead of you should be able to pass the baton to you. By communicating a clear and comprehensive direction, you should be able to trust the team and pass the baton. From there, it continues across disciplines and, finally, to everyone that engages with the completed creation. Being able to pass the baton with grace and humility is an important example that will be felt by the team. And it prepares the next generation of creatives to continue forward upon the foundation established.

An often-repeated phrase of people in support of specific disciplines is to always try and make yourself irrelevant. Beyond strengthening the team to learn and execute on what you already know, it frees you up to tackle new challenges. And there will always be new challenges. But it is important to embrace this by sharing everything you have learned, both successes and failures. All too often, we share only the positive outcomes, ignoring the stumbles and missteps that helped us arrive at our ultimate destination. Some of this is human nature and some of it is PR and marketing-driven motives to not show anything but a perfect production process. But that does everyone a disservice by not showing the lessons that needed to be learned from the mistakes that were made. Because not all lessons learned are the correct ones. So the mistakes need to be equally shared. That allows people to see if the lessons apply to the problems they encounter. And think about other possible solutions to mistakes that may be coming in the future.

Which leaves us with the *Post Project Survey*.[4] This survey feeds into the Team Size Calculator, as discussed in Chapter 5. This survey is for people to fill out when they have shipped a game. At its core, the survey is set up so that it will spit out a sheet that can be easily copy/pasted into the team size document. But it expands the animation tech disciplines to track leadership and external development happening in that realm. It also has an additional section that asks questions around overtime, communication, turnover and iteration speed.

The intent of this is to have standardized, per-project data that can be accessed by the community and can then also be cross-checked against the annual *AnimState of the Industry Survey* in all of these regards. All of which is meant to get people to share mistakes, successes, struggles and satisfactions. Because ultimately, the more we all know, the more we can create an intentional direction for others to build upon.

NOTES

1 I learned of Mikhail Bakhtin thanks to a brief conversation with Hannah Nicklin on a game dev discord server. I would love to say I read *Rabelais and His World*, which looks to be where the idea of carnival or folk festivities was properly explained. But I got as far as his Wikipedia entry to find these before immediately nodding my head and realizing this was at the heart of what I intend in the sort of communal team experiences.

2 As someone in a leadership and vision-setting role, it is important to fully understand how culture is influenced by your own personal bias and how that can be used in both good and bad ways. The good I have described here, but to see how culture and vision can be used as tools against fostering as creatively diverse a team as possible, I highly recommend reading *Culture is bad for you: Inequality in the cultural and creative* industries (Brook, O'Brien & Taylor, 2020), *Elite Capture: How the Powerful Took Over Identity Politics* (Táíwò, 2022) and *The Story Paradox: How Our Love of Storytelling Builds Societies and Tears them Down* (Gottschall, 2021).

3 While these questions, as stated in *Craig Ferguson: Does This Need to Be Said?* (2011), are not in this exact context, I do love how universal they can be in asking someone to step back and be intentional in both their reaction and response. But if you want something that isn't from a comedian, I suppose '*We have two ears and one mouth so that we can listen twice as much as we speak*' by Epictetus would fit the bill.

4 One final request is for you to always use the Post-Project Animation Team Survey, as found on AnimState, every time you wrap a project. The more we all share, the stronger and more knowledgeable we collectively become.

CHAPTER 13

Afterword

To BRING THIS BOOK full circle, here again is the quote from George Massenburg that occupies a constant place in my head.

'You have to work from your head, your heart and your guts... you have to figure out what is common to this... that balance.'

It feels like a large part of this book has been focused on translating the feelings of the heart and the gut into the language of the brain. Which is essentially logic and reason. That is at the core of most western philosophies, sciences and economics. And for an art form like animation within a medium like games, both of which have been so intrinsically tied to industry and business, I suppose that is to be expected in a book like this. But what I want to finish on is a plea to use this ability to communicate between the head, the heart and the gut to inform new, more interesting creations.

After the above quote, another reference that is always at the front of my mind is Peter Brook's *The Empty Space*, which is a collection of essays he wrote in the 1960s to describe his view of the state of theater at the time.[1] It is the first three he discusses about the Deadly, Holy and Rough, which most specifically and poignantly match the current state of game development.

Deadly represents the derivative, safe and business-driven creations that are often the focus of the industry. This is classified as Deadly because it is largely devoid of that creative spark of life. The sentiments of 'good enough' or 'this is how it has always been done' live within the Deadly. The continued reference or recreation of other work in an effort to provide

DOI: 10.1201/9781003356196-13

more of the same is what powers the Deadly. The Deadly is a blackhole that can be easy to surrender to and hard to escape. But escape it, we must. Which leads us to the other types.

One way to escape the gravitational pull of the Deadly is by committing to and scaling to the heights of the Holy. This is devoting yourself to execute the craft to such an exceptional level that it elevates even the deadliest of materials to become inspired. It pushes beyond what others thought was previously possible.

The other way out of the Deadly is towards the Rough. This is everything from the naïve amateur that doesn't know of established methods to someone making use of whatever is available at the time. Examples here can be everything from the vulgar, to the experimental, or to re-contextualizing Deadly works in an entirely new way.

For another way of looking at the Deadly, the Holy and the Rough, I like to think of them as this triangle (Figure 13.1).

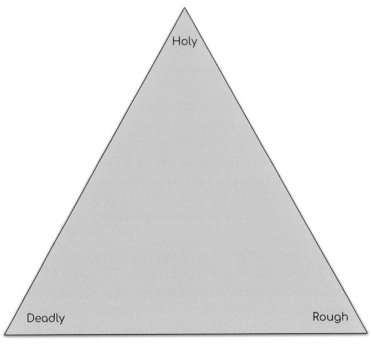

Inspired by Peter Brook's *The Empty Space*

FIGURE 13.1 A visualization of how I view what Peter Brook called the Deadly, Holy and Rough.

In this context, the Holy is climbing a steep mountain, and if you fall or don't climb high enough, you are still within the event horizon of the Deadly. The Rough you can more clearly walk towards, as the option to try anything different for the sake of being different is readily available. Though how successful that will be, like any creation, is reliant on the ability of the artist to communicate the intent behind what is so special about the Rough. And with any of these, there is also the person encountering the creation and their perception of what is being communicated.

Which is all to say, where on this triangle are you? Where is your project? Where do you wish you were? Where do the people you collaborate with think any of you or the project are? Where is the audience you are hoping to appeal to?

No one is going to intentionally place themselves in the Deadly. But remember that the Deadly is in fact a blackhole, always trying to pull in anything that crosses its' event horizon. Every 'good enough' is a step towards that black hole. Every business first decision, or thinking only with your head, is a step towards that black hole. Safe, 'by the book' creations are a path that almost always leads to the black hole. Every algorithm defined by the monoculture of the Deadly media grows the blackhole. And the only way to grow the triangle is by pushing ever further into the Holy and/or Rough.

Which is why clear intent in terms of expectations and vision is so important. It allows you, collectively, to pick a spot on that triangle, as far away from the deadly as you can all get to, and pull there with a singular direction and force. The glut of similar games is not because people are trying to aim for the Deadly. It is often because the team is pulling at different angles on this triangle. And without a singular pull at a unified angle, towards a singular point, everyone is playing an individual tug of war with a black hole.

This is where a dedication to a craft and understanding the value of each is something we should forever appreciate and champion.[2] This is where developing a sense of taste is important in refusing to feed the blackhole.[3] This is where the value of the auteur continues to be relevant, even when people who have been given the label find ways to abuse it.

Another way of looking at all of this is what art critic Manny Farber defines as White Elephant Art vs Termite Art.[4] White Elephant Art is that which is meant to look impressive but is lacking any unique creative intent. Whereas Termite Art is that which burrows, gnaws and claws at whatever is in front of it. Leaving only remnants of its existence in the form of whatever tunnels it carved and the detritus it left behind. The White Elephant Art can be hard to miss, as it demands your attention and can often find praise in people mistaking the ornate as valuable. But when you come across Termite Art, it can stick with you. You can feel the intense dedication and focus and marvel at how something so seemingly small or benign can make such a large impact.

Weaving together the thoughts of Peter Brook and Manny Farber, it is clear to see how White Elephant Art exists between the Deadly and the Holy. But to truly reach the summit of the Holy, or to venture to the Rough, we need to embrace our inner Termite. Because it is through the determination of the termite that we can escape the black hole. The effort of the director then becomes how to best point the colony of termites towards a shared objective.

Something a lot of people often cite as a method for this is the improv approach of saying 'Yes, and...' Which is a step in the right direction, but it is not going to guarantee a shared goal. 'Yes, and...' is great for brainstorming, but by its very nature, it is an exercise of the moment, with the side effect of being a short form of entertainment. If the creative, collaborative process stops at 'Yes, and..' everyone involved will lose focus and tire out. This is what happens all too often in pre-production, with everyone tired out at different creative locations, with an ultimate direction and deadline defined by the money left, which means 'Yes, and...' has burned creative good will and still not led to an intentional vision.

To apply this approach beyond the novelty of defining a possibility space, it needs to be focused on building the creative and collaborative muscles for full production. On a stage or set, even when improv is employed, there is not a random context of goals, objectives and relationships devised on the spot. Those are defined ahead of time and adjusted to the overarching needs in real time to deliver on the intent of the final creation. The best direction is to establish that context for everyone involved, with the leeway to add their own spin to it. And then adjust that spin in such a way that it propels the entire creation forward.[5]

That approach and intent have been at the heart of this book. Meet and understand everyone involved in the creation. Define the plates that need to be spinning. And make sure the right people are spinning the right plates at the right time. And then step back, watch the show and adjust accordingly.

Which is to say, don't use this book as a checklist, where checking off every box here will build a perfect foundation upon which to build a perfect creation. That is a path that will almost certainly lead to a sense of going through the motions, which will see your creation establish itself squarely in the Deadly. Think of everything in this book more as a set of tools and instructions on how to build a blueprint for the unique creation that only the team you are a part of can create. Because we need more Holy and Rough. We need more Termite Art. And I hope this book can help you realize more of each.

NOTES

1 Anyone that I talk to about the creative process for more than 5 minutes has probably heard me cite Peter Brook's *The Empty Space: A Book about the Theatre: Deadly, Holy, Rough, Immediate* (1968). To read something written over half a decade ago about a different creative field that perfectly reflects the current creative state of the game industry is a clear representation of both how circular and insular every creative industry seems to be.

2 Another shout out to Matthew B.Crawford's *Shop Class as Soulcraft: An Inquiry into the Value of Work* (2010). It turns out someone with a PhD in political philosophy who fixes motorcycles is the exact sort of person capable of speaking well about the value and need for a focus on crafts and trades.

3 As previously referenced in Chapter 3, Erik Hoel's 'The Intrinsic Perspective' posts are regular must-reads when I see them pop up in my inbox. But his 2022 post, *Exit the supersensorium*, looking at the current state of media through the lens of neuroscience, dreams and fostering a sense of taste, is especially well worth your time.

4 When discussing my obsession with Peter Brooks' *The Empty Space*, as well as B-movies, with James Fagan, a co-worker at Compulsion games, he mentioned a similarity in thought with Manny Farber's *White Elephant Art vs Termite Art* essay (Film Culture, No.27, Winter 1962–63). The fact Farber specifically cites Howard Hawks in the essay, who was previously cited in Chapter 9, in regards to quality being *'three good scenes and no bad ones'* feels like a wonderful coincidence to help wrap up this book.

5 Here again, I will recommend Rob Austin and Lee Devin's *Artful Making: What Managers Need to Know about How Artists Work* (2003) as a perfect deep dive into the approach of thinking of production leadership in terms of theater. What I have tried here to convey in paragraphs, they expertly explain over chapters.

Acknowledgments

This book exists thanks to the conversations, learnings, opportunities and experiences made possible by so many people. Without them, I would certainly be creating from within the deadly. If I was creating anything at all.

To my wife Leslie, who regularly inspires me by her ability and desire to always learn new crafts, search out new experiences and never be content with good enough in anything she sets her mind and focus on.

To the many mentors I have had the fortune of learning from, both directly and indirectly. Your open sharing of knowledge and experiences provided me with the seeds and tools to grow the learnings I share in this book. Thank you, Ed Hooks, Tim Borrelli, Ryan Duffin, Simon Unger, Jay Hosfelt, Tasha Sounart, Paul McComas, Jonathan Cooper, Matthew Goldman, Anoop Shekar, Gwen Frey, Mariel Cartwright, Billy Harper, Erik Medina, Almudena Soria Sancho, Jeremy Yates, Bruno Velazquez and Alexander Drouin. You have each been perfectly timed sources and models of inspiration and reason throughout my career and creative development.

To all of my creative conspirators, many of the ideas in this book are direct results of your helping to talk through, test and apply everything in here to be more than theories. Sometimes in depth or even just in passing. Your willingness to engage with and discuss the random topics and inspirations at the heart of this book made it so much better than it would have been otherwise. Thank you, Lana Bachynski (also the amazing cover artist!), Esther Ko, Frank Gordon, Ju Li Khaw, Kristjan Zadziuk, Jalil Sadool, Dan Lowe, Lee Dowsett, John Paul Rhinemiller, Darren Randall, Jake Clark, Lyndsey Pendley, Zach Lowery, Nawwaf Barakat, Lacey Bannister, Carl Boulay, Nathan Zufelt, Sol Brennan and Adam Clark. Each of you is inspiring in how much you share your expertise and collaborate with everyone around you. You make better any endeavor you are a part of.

Thank you to everyone I have ever worked with, who has agreed to speak at the Animation Exchange and GDC Animation Bootcamp/Summit, has contributed to AnimState, is a member of the AnimState community and has invited me to speak at conferences or organizations you are a part of. There are far too many of you to list, but I am sure when reading this, you have seen nuggets of our discussions throughout. And the next time we see one another, I look forward to further polishing those nuggets.

I would have no career or experience if not for my family, who inspire and support my creative future. To my mother, Brenda Jungbluth, and my grandparents, Harriet and William Porter, who not only supported but also encouraged my interest in art. There was no reason to think there was ever a future in which I could be doing what I am now doing, but that never stopped them from dreaming with me. To my Aunt and Uncle, Twila and Dave Hummel, who gave me regular opportunities to cover papers and walls with my art. And my sister, Sara Jungbluth, who still keeps me honest.

To the people in college who helped me realize the depths of my potential: Craig Tiede, Henry Frew, Scott Hafner, Steve Carpenter and Michael Genz. Each of you helped me to see and grow the different skills and approaches I now rely on every day.

And finally, thank you to everyone at CRC Press/Taylor and Francis, for making this book real. Thank you, Sean Connelly and Danielle Zarfati, for giving me the opportunity to write this book and supporting its creation.

Index

Note: *Italic* page numbers refer to figures and page numbers followed by "n" denote endnotes.